ANIMAL ENCYCLOPEDIAS

THE AUSTRALIAN ANIMAL ENCYCLOPEDIA

BY HANNAH GRAMSON

Encyclopedias

An Imprint of Abdo Reference
abdobooks.com

TABLE OF CONTENTS

WELCOME TO AUSTRALIA 4
- Australian Habitats 6
- The Great Barrier Reef 8

MAMMALS 10
LAND MAMMALS 12
- Black Flying-Fox 12
- Brushtail Possum 13
- Dingo 14
- Dromedary Camel 16
- Echidna 17
- Fat-Tailed Dunnart 18
- Greater Bilby 19
- Kangaroo 20
- Koala 22
- Numbat 24
- Pademelon 25
- Platypus 26
- Quokka 28
- Quoll 30
- Red Fox 31
- Sugar Glider 32
- Tasmanian Devil 34
- Tree Kangaroo 35
- Wallaby 36
- Wallaroo 37
- Wombat 38

MARINE MAMMALS 40
- Australian Fur Seal 40
- Australian Humpback Dolphin 41
- Australian Sea Lion 42
- Blue Whale 44
- Bottlenose Dolphin 45
- Dugong 46
- Humpback Whale 48
- Leopard Seal 50
- Long-Finned Pilot Whale 51
- Melon-Headed Whale 52
- Minke Whale 53
- Orca 54
- Southern Right Whale 56
- Sperm Whale 57

ADDITIONAL MAMMALS 58

REPTILES AND AMPHIBIANS 60
CROCODILES 62
- Freshwater Crocodile 62
- Saltwater Crocodile 64

FROGS 66
- Crucifix Frog 66
- Green and Golden Bell Frog 67
- Magnificent Tree Frog 68
- Red-Eyed Tree Frog 69
- Southern Corroboree Frog 70
- Turtle Frog 72

LIZARDS 74
- Australian Water Dragon 74
- Barking Gecko 76
- Bearded Dragon 77
- Blue-Tongued Skink 78
- Boyd's Forest Dragon 79
- Central Netted Dragon 80
- Cunningham's Skink 81
- Frilled Lizard 82
- Lace Monitor 84
- Painted Dragon 85
- Perentie 86
- Shingleback Lizard 88
- Southern Leaf-Tailed Gecko 89
- Thorny Devil 90

RIVER TURTLES 92
- Pig-Nosed Turtle 92
- Red-Bellied Short-Necked Turtle 93
- Snake-Necked Turtle 94

SEA TURTLES 96
- Flatback Sea Turtle 96
- Green Sea Turtle 97
- Hawksbill Turtle 98
- Leatherback Turtle 99
- Loggerhead Sea Turtle 100
- Olive Ridley Turtle 101

SNAKES **102**
  Australian Scrub Python 102
  Bandy-Bandy Snake 104
  Black-Headed Python 105
  Common Death Adder................................ 106
  Eastern Brown Snake 107
  Green Tree Python 108
  Inland Taipan 110
  Lowland Copperhead 111
  Mulga Snake 112
  Red-Bellied Black Snake 113
  Small-Eyed Snake 114
  Tiger Snake 115
  Yellow-Bellied Sea Snake 116
  Yellow-Faced Whip Snake 117

ADDITIONAL REPTILES AND AMPHIBIANS **118**

BIRDS **120**
  Australian Bustard 122
  Australian King Parrot 123
  Australian Ringneck 124
  Barking Owl 125
  Black Swan 126
  Brolga 128
  Budgerigar 129
  Cassowary 130
  Emu 132
  Galah 133
  Gouldian Finch 134
  Laughing Kookaburra 135
  Little Penguin 136
  Peregrine Falcon 138
  Regent Bowerbird 139
  Splendid Fairy-Wren 140
  Tawny Frogmouth 141
  Wedge-Tailed Eagle 142
  Yellow-Tailed Black Cockatoo 143

ADDITIONAL BIRDS **144**

FISH AND OTHER MARINE LIFE **146**
  Australian Giant Cuttlefish 148
  Barrier Reef Anemonefish 150
  Bluespotted Fantail Ray 151
  Common Sydney Octopus 152
  Giant Clam 154
  Great White Shark 156
  Hammerhead Shark 158
  Hoodwinker Sunfish 159
  Leafy Seadragon 160
  Manta Ray 162
  Māori Wrasse 164
  Spotted Handfish 165
  Tiger Shark 166
  Weedy Seadragon 167
  Whale Shark 168

ADDITIONAL FISH AND OTHER MARINE LIFE ... **170**

INSECTS AND SPIDERS **172**
  Australian Tarantula 174
  Cabbage White Butterfly 176
  Cairns Birdwing Butterfly 177
  Christmas Beetle 178
  Giant Burrowing Cockroach 179
  Giant Prickly Stick Insect 180
  Giant Water Bug 181
  Goliath Stick Insect 182
  Hercules Moth 183
  Triangular Spider 184
  Ulysses Butterfly 185

ADDITIONAL INSECTS AND SPIDERS **186**

GLOSSARY **188**

TO LEARN MORE **189**

INDEX **190**

PHOTO CREDITS **191**

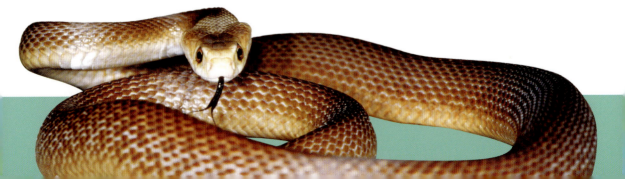

WELCOME TO AUSTRALIA

With area of nearly three million square miles (7,769,964.3 sq km), Australia is one of the largest countries in the world. It's also the only country to cover an entire continent. Australia is located south of Asia, between the Indian Ocean and the Pacific Ocean.

Because Australia is isolated, its ecosystem is unique. The country is home to many animal species that aren't found anywhere else in the world. It's also home to many of the world's deadliest species.

Shrublands in Australia

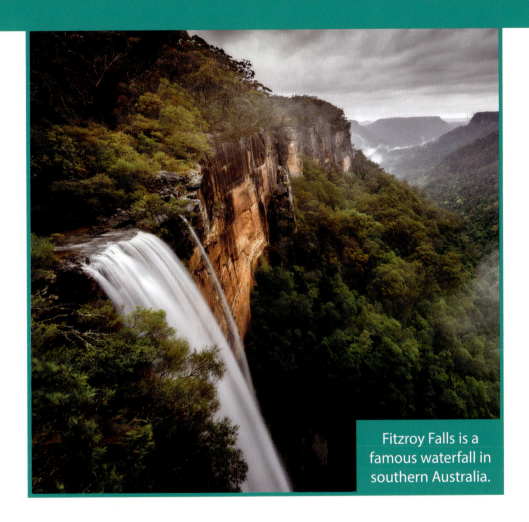

Fitzroy Falls is a famous waterfall in southern Australia.

The climate varies greatly across Australia. Northern Australia has a humid, tropical climate. Southern Australia's climate is temperate, with mild weather year-round. Central Australia, known as the Australian Outback, is arid or semiarid desert. It covers more than one-third of the country. Few people live in this region of the country.

AUSTRALIAN HABITATS

Many different kinds of habitats can be found in Australia. These include grasslands, savannas, shrublands, forests, woodlands, deserts, and heath. There are also many freshwater habitats, such as lakes, rivers, ponds, and wetlands.

Central and western Australia are largely made up of deserts, shrublands, and grasslands. Deserts are dry areas with little vegetation. Grasslands, savannas, shrublands, and heath are wide open areas with short vegetation. These places usually don't receive much precipitation.

Australia has eight different types of forests, including rainforests. Most of Australia's forests are found in the east. Woodlands are areas where trees are spread farther apart, often separated by heath or grassland. Most of Australia's woodlands are found in the south.

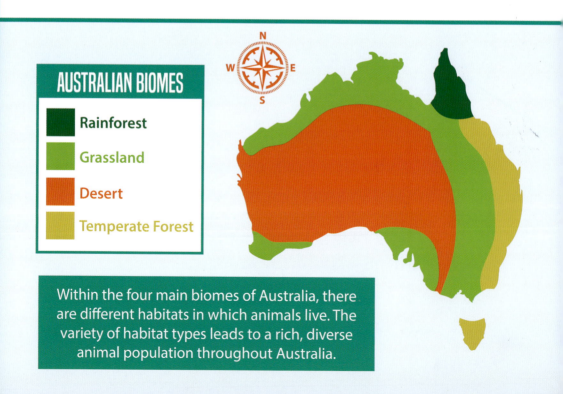

Within the four main biomes of Australia, there are different habitats in which animals live. The variety of habitat types leads to a rich, diverse animal population throughout Australia.

The Daintree River winds through forest in North Queensland, Australia.

Port Campbell National Park is in southern Australia.

This desert is in Kanku-Breakaways Conservation Park in South Australia.

WELCOME TO AUSTRALIA

Six of the world's seven species of sea turtles live in the Great Barrier Reef.

THE GREAT BARRIER REEF

Off the northeastern coast of Australia is the Great Barrier Reef, the largest coral reef in the world. The Great Barrier Reef is a long, narrow formation of coral. It runs parallel to Australia's shoreline and is mostly underwater. It's about 1,430 miles (2,301.4 km) long, making it the largest structure made of living organisms on Earth.

The Great Barrier Reef formed over millions of years. It's made up of the bone-like remains of millions of tiny corals, a type of invertebrate. Despite its name, the Great Barrier Reef isn't one large reef, but rather a group of about 3,000 individual reefs.

The Great Barrier Reef is home to more than 9,000 known animal species. This includes about 130 species of sharks and rays, 3,000 species of mollusks, 30 species of mammals, and 1,625 species of fish.

An aerial view shows part of the Great Barrier Reef.

MAMMALS

There are more than 6,000 species of mammals throughout the world. They're found on every continent and in every ocean. They live in a wide range of habitats and vary in size. Some are tiny, such as the bumblebee bat, which only grows to be about one inch (2.5 cm). Others are enormous, such as the blue whale, which can grow to be more than 100 feet (30.5 m) long.

All mammals breathe air and have a spine. They are also warm-blooded, which means they can keep their body at roughly the same temperature regardless of their surroundings.

Dingoes are also called warragals.

The babies of nearly all mammals grow inside their mother's body. Marsupials are a type of mammal that give birth to their babies while they're still developing. The baby will climb into a pouch or fold on its mother's back or stomach and stay there until it's developed fully. More than half Australia's mammals are marsupials. Australia also has two species of unique mammals called monotremes, which lay eggs.

FUN FACT
Humans are mammals too.

Western grey kangaroos are one of four species of kangaroo in Australia.

Echidnas roll into a ball when they are in danger.

MAMMALS
LAND MAMMALS

BLACK FLYING-FOX

ALL ABOUT
Black flying-foxes have short, black fur and can have reddish-brown rings around their eyes and neck. They are nocturnal, traveling up to 31 miles (49.9 km) per night in search of food.
- **Length:** 6 to 7.5 inches (15.2 to 19.1 cm)
- **Weight:** 1.1 to 2.2 pounds (0.5 to 1 kg)
- **Lifespan:** up to 4.5 years
- **Conservation Status:** Least Concern

HABITAT & DIET
Black flying-foxes live mainly in rainforests, eucalyptus forests, and savanna woodlands in northern or eastern Australia. They often roost in bamboo. Their diet consists of fruit, nectar, and pollen.

FAMILY & SOCIAL LIFE
Black flying-foxes roost in large colonies, called camps. These can have hundreds of thousands of bats, but most camps have less than 30,000.

FUN FACT
The wingspan of a black flying-fox is about 3 feet (0.9 m).

BRUSHTAIL POSSUM

ALL ABOUT

About the size of house cats, brushtail possums have a pointed nose, big ears, and a long, bushy tail. Their sharp claws help them climb trees.

- **Length:** 13.5 to 21.5 inches (34.3 to 54.6 cm)
- **Weight:** 2.7 to 10 pounds (1.2 to 4.5 kg)
- **Lifespan:** 10 to 12 years
- **Conservation Status:** Least Concern

HABITAT & DIET

Brushtail possums are found in forests and woodlands across Australia. During the day, they sleep in hollow logs, tree trunks, or on branches. At night, they feast on leaves, blossoms, fruit, and sometimes insects.

FAMILY & SOCIAL LIFE

Brushtail possums live alone, except when they're mating. If two possums meet at night, they will avoid each other.

DID YOU KNOW?

Brushtail possums in cold climates usually have black or gray fur. In warmer climates, they have copper-colored fur.

DINGO

ALL ABOUT

Dingoes are wild dogs with a bushy tail and white feet. The color of their fur can vary. Dingoes who live in sandy areas often have yellow fur, whereas dingoes who live in forested areas might have dark tan or brown fur.

- **Length:** 34 to 48 inches (86.4 to 121.9 cm)
- **Weight:** 26 to 43 pounds (11.8 to 19.5 kg)
- **Lifespan:** 7 to 10 years
- **Conservation Status:** Vulnerable

HABITAT & DIET

Dingoes can live in many different habitats, but they prefer woodlands and grassland areas. Dingoes are apex predators, which means they are at the top of their food chain. They mainly eat mammals such as rabbits, kangaroos, wallabies, and wombats but will also eat reptiles and birds.

FAMILY & SOCIAL LIFE

Dingoes live in packs of about 10 members that travel and hunt together. Dingoes rarely bark. Instead, they communicate with each other through howling, especially at night. They might rub or urinate on objects to mark their territory.

Only the dominant members of a dingo pack have a litter, which usually consists of five pups. The other members of the pack help take care of the young.

> **FUN FACT**
> Dingoes are Australia's largest carnivore.

DID YOU KNOW?

Dingoes have lived in Australia for at least 3,500 years. They may have been brought to the country by seafarers from Southeast Asia.

MAMMALS: LAND MAMMALS

DROMEDARY CAMEL

ALL ABOUT

Dromedary camels were first brought to Australia in 1840. Now, with more than one million feral camels in the country, they are considered an invasive species.

- **Length:** 7 to 11 feet (2.1 to 3.4 m)
- **Weight:** 880 to 1,320 pounds (399.2 to 598.7 kg)
- **Lifespan:** up to 40 years
- **Conservation Status:** Not Assessed

DID YOU KNOW?

Dromedary camels can close their nostrils to prevent sand from getting in their noses during sandstorms.

HABITAT & DIET

Dromedary camels live mainly in central Australia, where they are well suited to the dry desert climate. They are herbivores, eating mostly thorny plants, dry grasses, and saltbush.

FAMILY & SOCIAL LIFE

Dromedary camels live in groups of 2 to 20 camels. Usually only one camel in a group is male. Camels travel single file, with the male directing the group from behind.

ECHIDNA

ALL ABOUT

Echidnas are covered in sharp spines. They have a long nose, sometimes called a beak, that they use to sniff out prey.

- **Length:** 14 to 30 inches (35.6 to 76.2 cm)
- **Weight:** 10 to 13 pounds (4.5 to 5.9 kg)
- **Lifespan:** up to 10 years
- **Conservation Status:** Varies by subspecies

> **DID YOU KNOW?**
> Echidnas are named after a monster from Greek mythology.

HABITAT & DIET

Echidnas can live in a wide range of habitats, including woodlands, scrublands, deserts, and grasslands. They use their long, sticky tongue to eat ants and termites, their main source of food.

FAMILY & SOCIAL LIFE

Echidnas mostly live alone, except during mating season. Females usually lay just one grape-sized egg per year. The mother keeps it in her pouch for 10 days before the baby hatches.

FAT-TAILED DUNNART

ALL ABOUT
Fat-tailed dunnarts are tiny, mouse like marsupials. They store body fat in their long tail. When a lot of food is available, their tail is fat.
- **Length:** 2.5 to 4 inches (6.4 to 10.2 cm)
- **Weight:** 0.4 to 0.7 ounces (11.3 to 19.8 g)
- **Lifespan:** up to 1.5 years
- **Conservation Status:** Least Concern

DID YOU KNOW?
Fat-tailed dunnarts are one of 19 different species of dunnarts found in Australia.

HABITAT & DIET
Fat-tailed dunnarts live in a wide range of habitats, including woodlands and shrublands. They are carnivores, dining on spiders, worms, and a variety of insects.

FAMILY & SOCIAL LIFE
Between 8 and 10 fat-tailed dunnarts are born at one time. The mother carries her babies in a pouch for about 60 days after they're born.

GREATER BILBY

ALL ABOUT

Greater bilbies are tiny marsupials with long, blue-gray fur, a short tail, and large ears. To protect themselves from predators and daytime heat, greater bilbies dig spiral-shaped burrows that can be up to 9 feet (2.7 m) long and 6 feet (1.8 m) deep.

- **Length:** 11 to 21.5 inches (27.9 to 54.6 cm)
- **Weight:** 2.2 to 5.5 pounds (1 to 2.5 kg)
- **Lifespan:** up to 7 years
- **Conservation Status:** Vulnerable

HABITAT & DIET

Greater bilbies primarily live in shrublands, woodlands, and areas with dry, rocky soil. They are nocturnal, feasting mainly on seeds, fungi, fruit, and insects such as termites.

FAMILY & SOCIAL LIFE

Greater bilbies usually live alone, except when mating.

DID YOU KNOW?

There was another species of bilby called the lesser bilby that was extinct by 1960.

MAMMALS: LAND MAMMALS

KANGAROO

ALL ABOUT

Kangaroos are the world's largest marsupial. The color of their fur ranges from reddish brown to gray. Their long tail and large feet help them balance and jump long distances.

There are four different types of kangaroos: red, eastern gray, western gray, and antilopine. Red kangaroos are the largest and most common.

- **Length:** 3 to 8 feet (0.9 to 2.4 m)
- **Weight:** up to 200 pounds (90.7 kg)
- **Lifespan:** up to 23 years
- **Conservation Status:** Least Concern

HABITAT & DIET

Kangaroos can be found in woods, bushlands, grasslands, savannas, and scrublands. Kangaroos are herbivores, dining on grasses, leaves, flowers, fruit, and moss.

DID YOU KNOW?

Kangaroos can leap nearly 30 feet (9.1 m) in a single jump. They can travel more than 40 miles per hour (64.4 kmh).

FUN FACT
There are more kangaroos in Australia than humans.

FAMILY & SOCIAL LIFE
Kangaroos live in small groups, called herds, mobs, or troops, of up to 100 animals. They often touch noses or sniff one another to build bonds.

Female kangaroos carry their babies, called joeys, in their pouch. When a joey is first born, it's about the size of a grape. For the first 10 months of its life, a joey stays in its mother's pouch, only leaving for short periods of time to graze on grasses.

KOALA

ALL ABOUT
Koalas are sometimes mistakenly called koala bears. But koalas aren't bears. They're marsupials. Koalas climb trees using sharp claws and opposable thumbs. They clean their coarse fur using two toes on their feet that are fused together, called a grooming claw.
- **Length:** 2 to 3 feet (0.6 to 0.9 m)
- **Weight:** 9 to 31 pounds (4.1 to 14.1 kg)
- **Lifespan:** 10 to 12 years
- **Conservation Status:** Vulnerable

HABITAT & DIET
Koalas spend most of their time high in eucalyptus trees in eastern Australia. They sleep up to 20 hours a day. Koalas only eat eucalyptus leaves and will consume about 1 pound (0.5 kg) per day. Eucalyptus leaves have toxins that are poisonous to most animals, but koalas have a special digestive system that breaks down the toxins.

FAMILY & SOCIAL LIFE
Koalas are mostly solitary, but they will live in trees near other koalas. Female koalas give birth to one joey at a time. The joey further develops in the mother's pouch for about six months. The joey will then come out for short periods, spending time riding on its mother's stomach or back.

DID YOU KNOW?

A fossil from 100,000 years ago suggests koalas were once the size of full-grown bulls.

FUN FACT

Koalas have two thumbs on each hand.

NUMBAT

ALL ABOUT
Numbats are small mammals with grayish-brown or reddish fur, long claws, and a bushy tail.
- **Length:** 7 to 12 inches (17.8 to 30.5 cm)
- **Weight:** 14 to 25 ounces (396.9 to 708.7 g)
- **Lifespan:** 4 to 5 years
- **Conservation Status:** Endangered

DID YOU KNOW?
Numbats have eyes on either side of their head. This helps them watch for predators.

HABITAT & DIET
Numbats make their homes in hollow logs or underground burrows in southern and western Australia. Numbats use their long, thin tongue to reach into small holes to collect termites, their only source of food. Numbats eat up to 20,000 termites a day.

FAMILY & SOCIAL LIFE
Numbats usually live alone unless they're mating or taking care of a baby. Female numbats usually give birth to four babies at a time.

PADEMELON

ALL ABOUT
Pademelons are marsupials with reddish-brown or black fur, large hind feet, and a short tail.
- **Length:** 9 to 26 inches (22.9 to 66 cm)
- **Weight:** 10 to 40 pounds (4.5 to 18.1 kg)
- **Lifespan:** 5 to 9 years
- **Conservation Status:** Varies by species

FUN FACT
If a predator is nearby, pademelons might warn each other by thumping the ground with their back feet.

HABITAT & DIET
Pademelons are mostly found in dense areas of rainforests, eucalyptus forests, and grasslands of northeastern Australia. They're herbivores, eating mainly grasses, leaves, roots, and sometimes fruit.

FAMILY & SOCIAL LIFE
Pademelons live alone but sometimes gather in groups while eating. They communicate with each other through clucking sounds.

PLATYPUS

ALL ABOUT

With a flat tail, waterproof fur, webbed feet, and a duck-like bill, platypuses are one of the more unique-looking mammals on Earth. Platypuses are also one of the few venomous mammals. Although not fatal, their venom can cause severe pain and swelling.

- **Length:** 14.5 to 25 inches (36.8 to 63.5 cm)
- **Weight:** 2.2 to 6.6 pounds (1 to 3 kg)
- **Lifespan:** up to 20 years
- **Conservation Status:** Near Threatened

HABITAT & DIET

Platypuses are designed for semiaquatic life, living in and around freshwater habitats, including rivers, streams, and lakes in eastern Australia. Platypuses use electroreceptors in their bill to detect prey such as shrimp, insects, or tadpoles. They use hard mouth pads, rather than teeth, to grind their food.

FAMILY & SOCIAL LIFE

Platypuses usually live alone, although several might live in the same body of water. A female platypus lays one to three eggs at a time.

FUN FACT
Baby platypuses are called puggles.

DID YOU KNOW?
Male platypuses deliver venom through the spurs in their hind limbs.

QUOKKA

ALL ABOUT

Quokkas are sometimes called the "happiest animal in the world" because their face muscles and front teeth make them look like they're smiling. These marsupials have coarse, brownish-gray hair covering most of their body, small front paws, and large hind feet.

- **Length:** 16 to 21 inches (40.6 to 53.3 cm)
- **Weight:** 6 to 10 pounds (2.7 to 4.5 kg)
- **Lifespan:** about 10 years
- **Conservation Status:** Vulnerable

HABITAT & DIET

Quokkas are usually found in shrublands, wetlands, and forests of southwestern Australia. They prefer warmer climates but build their homes in thickets or other places that are cool and shady during the day. Quokkas are herbivores, dining on many different types of grasses and leaves.

FAMILY & SOCIAL LIFE

Quokkas are nocturnal, spending the night looking for food alone or in small groups. Like other marsupials, babies are carried in their mother's pouch for about 6 months until they find their own home range at 12 to 18 months old.

DID YOU KNOW?

Quokkas don't have any natural defenses. They create trails through vegetation to escape from predators, which include dingoes and birds of prey.

FUN FACT
Quokkas store fat in their tail.

QUOLL

ALL ABOUT
Quolls have black or brown fur with white spots, a pointed snout, and a long tail.

- **Length:** 16 to 21 inches (40.6 to 53.3 cm)
- **Weight:** up to 11 pounds (5 kg)
- **Lifespan:** 2 to 4 years
- **Conservation Status:** Varies by species

HABITAT & DIET
Quolls are found in coastal heath, woodlands, and forests. Quolls are carnivores. Smaller quolls eat insects, reptiles, frogs, and small birds and mammals. Larger quolls eat medium-sized birds and mammals such as possums and rabbits.

FAMILY & SOCIAL LIFE
Quolls mostly live alone, except when mating or taking care of babies.

DID YOU KNOW?
When two quolls are near each other, they might hiss or scream at one another.

RED FOX

ALL ABOUT

Red foxes have yellowish-red to reddish-brown fur, large ears, and a bushy tail. First brought to Australia by Europeans in the 1850s for hunting purposes, they are now found throughout the country.

- **Length:** 2 to 3 feet (0.6 to 0.9 m)
- **Weight:** 9 to 17.5 pounds (4.1 to 7.9 kg)
- **Lifespan:** 3 to 5 years
- **Conservation Status:** Least Concern

DID YOU KNOW?

Foxes often bury food in the ground to save it for later.

HABITAT & DIET

Red foxes can live in a wide range of habitats, including grasslands, forests, and deserts. They're omnivores, but their diet largely consists of rabbits, mice, frogs, and birds.

FAMILY & SOCIAL LIFE

Red foxes are mostly solitary but can form groups during mating season.

SUGAR GLIDER

ALL ABOUT

Sugar gliders are small marsupials that are known for their ability to soar through the air. Their "wings," called patagia, are made of thin skin stretching from their front paws to their back ankles.

A sugar glider uses its wide field of vision to determine distances before launching. Once airborne, it steers by tilting its body and using its tail like a rudder.

- **Length:** 6 to 8 inches (15.2 to 20.3 cm)
- **Weight:** 3.4 to 5.6 ounces (96 to 159 g)
- **Lifespan:** 3 to 9 years
- **Conservation Status:** Least Concern

FUN FACT

Sugar gliders can "fly" about 165 feet (50.3 m) at one time.

MAMMALS: LAND MAMMALS

HABITAT & DIET

Sugar gliders live in forests of eastern Australia, Tasmania, and nearby islands. They rarely descend from the trees. These nocturnal omnivores eat a range of plants, pollen, nectar, and tree sap, as well as insects and small lizards.

DID YOU KNOW?

Sugar gliders have become popular in the pet trade, but, like most wildlife, they do not make good pets. In many places, it is illegal to own a sugar glider.

FAMILY & SOCIAL LIFE

Sugar gliders are social animals, usually forming groups of about seven adults, along with their babies. They are able to recognize one another through scents, which are unique to each individual. These marsupials communicate through a wide range of vocalizations including hissing, barking, and purring.

TASMANIAN DEVIL

ALL ABOUT

Tasmanian devils have coarse brown or black fur, with long front legs and short hind legs. They are the world's largest carnivorous marsupial.

- **Length:** 23 to 26 inches (58.4 to 66 cm)
- **Weight:** 9 to 26 pounds (4.1 to 11.8 kg)
- **Lifespan:** 5 to 8 years
- **Conservation Status:** Endangered

DID YOU KNOW?

Tasmanian devils gained a reputation for having a bad temper. But their aggressive behavior comes from fear rather than anger. When feeling threatened, they often bare their teeth and screech, hiss, or growl.

HABITAT & DIET

Tasmanian devils are only found on the island of Tasmania. They live in eucalyptus forests, woodlands, and shrublands. Mostly scavengers, they use their strong jaws and teeth to tear through animal carcasses, including the bones. Tasmanian devils primarily feast on birds, frogs, insects, and fish.

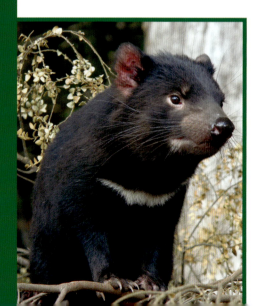

FAMILY & SOCIAL LIFE

Tasmanian devils mostly live alone but will often share an animal carcass with a group.

FUN FACT

Tasmanian devils produce a bad smell when they're under stress.

TREE KANGAROO

ALL ABOUT
Unlike most marsupials, tree kangaroos have arms and hind legs that are about the same size. Their strong front limbs help them easily climb trees.

- **Length:** 17 to 30 inches (43.2 to 76.2 cm)
- **Weight:** 15 to 30 pounds (6.8 to 13.6 kg)
- **Lifespan:** 8 to 14 years
- **Conservation Status:** Varies by species

HABITAT & DIET
Tree kangaroos usually live in tropical forests of northeastern Australia, where they spend most of their time up in trees. They eat mostly fruit and leaves.

FAMILY & SOCIAL LIFE
Tree kangaroos usually live alone, although some might share the same tree. They're mostly nocturnal, foraging for food at night and sleeping during the day.

FUN FACT
Tree kangaroos are the largest tree-dwelling mammals in Australia.

MAMMALS: LAND MAMMALS

WALLABY

ALL ABOUT

Wallabies are small kangaroo-like animals. They have large hind feet that help them bound long distances.
- **Length:** 12 to 41 inches (30.5 to 104.1 cm)
- **Weight:** up to 53 pounds (24 kg)
- **Lifespan:** up to 9 years
- **Conservation Status:** Varies by species

HABITAT & DIET

Wallabies live in different habitats, depending on their species. They can live in areas with rocky terrain or in coastal heath, swamps, and forests. Wallabies are herbivores, eating mainly grasses and plants.

FAMILY & SOCIAL LIFE

Most species of wallabies live alone, but some eat in small groups. If they feel threatened, wallabies might thump their feet on the ground to alert others.

> **FUN FACT**
> A wallaby's long tail helps it balance.

WALLAROO

ALL ABOUT

Wallaroos are marsupials larger than wallabies but smaller than kangaroos. They have shaggy, reddish-brown to dark gray fur with a large tail and hind feet.

- **Length:** 2.5 to 4.5 feet (0.8 to 1.4 m)
- **Weight:** 62 to 132 pounds (28.1 to 59.9 kg)
- **Lifespan:** up to 18 years
- **Conservation Status:** Varies by species

HABITAT & DIET

Found throughout Australia, wallaroos usually live in mountainous areas but are sometimes found in shrublands too. They are herbivores that primarily eat grasses and shrubs.

FAMILY & SOCIAL LIFE

Wallaroos usually live alone but sometimes form groups if food is abundant. Most social interaction among wallaroos occurs between a mother and her babies.

FUN FACT

Wallaroos can survive up to three months without drinking water.

MAMMALS: LAND MAMMALS

WOMBAT

ALL ABOUT
There are three species of wombat: the common wombat, the northern hairy-nosed wombat, and the southern hairy-nosed wombat. Wombats are medium-sized marsupials with a round body, short legs, and sharp claws used for digging.
- **Length:** 28 to 47 inches (71.1 to 119.4 cm)
- **Weight:** up to 88 pounds (39.9 kg)
- **Lifespan:** 5 to 15 years
- **Conservation Status:** Varies by species

HABITAT & DIET
Wombats live in underground burrows connected by tunnels. They are found in a wide range of southeastern Australian habitats, including grasslands, mountains, and forests. Wombats are nocturnal herbivores, dining on grasses, roots, and shrubs. It takes wombats 8 to 14 days to digest their food, and they can go years without drinking any water.

FAMILY & SOCIAL LIFE
Wombats mostly live alone but sometimes share their burrows with 10 or more individuals. However, they are territorial when it comes to feeding grounds. They spend up to 16 hours a day sleeping.

FUN FACT
Wombat poop is cube shaped.

Dingoes, eagles, and Tasmanian devils are some of the wombat's natural predators. When chased by a predator, wombats will escape into their underground burrows.

DID YOU KNOW?

Wombats have large front teeth that keep growing throughout their lifetime. Gnawing on tough plants prevents their teeth from getting too big.

MAMMALS
MARINE MAMMALS

AUSTRALIAN FUR SEAL

ALL ABOUT
Australian fur seals have a thick brownish-gray coat, long whiskers, and sharp teeth. Male Australian fur seals are two to three times the size of females.

- **Length:** 4.6 to 7.5 feet (1.4 to 2.3 m)
- **Weight:** 77 to 243 pounds (34.9 to 110.2 kg)
- **Lifespan:** 12 to 30 years
- **Conservation Status:** Least Concern

HABITAT & DIET
Australian fur seals are found in the ocean near southeastern Australia but often visit rocky islands and pebble beaches. Australian fur seals dine on a variety of bony fish, octopuses, and squid.

DID YOU KNOW?
Australian fur seals can dive more than 650 feet (198.1 m) underwater to catch food.

FAMILY & SOCIAL LIFE
Australian fur seals will come ashore to form breeding colonies called rookeries. Rookeries include one male and about 40 females.

AUSTRALIAN HUMPBACK DOLPHIN

ALL ABOUT
Australian humpback dolphins have a long rostrum and a small hump at the base of their dorsal fin.
- **Length:** up to 9 feet (2.7 m)
- **Weight:** up to 573 pounds (259.9 kg)
- **Lifespan:** 30 to more than 40 years
- **Conservation Status:** Vulnerable

FUN FACT
The dorsal fin on an Australian humpback dolphin can become floppy as it gets older.

HABITAT & DIET
Australian humpback dolphins are mainly found off the coast of northern Australia. They often stay near estuaries, rocky reefs, or in sheltered bays. Humpback dolphins eat a variety of fish, squid, and rays.

FAMILY & SOCIAL LIFE
Australian humpback dolphins tend to form groups of about four or five individuals, which are usually the same gender. They use whistles and clicking sounds to communicate and echolocate.

AUSTRALIAN SEA LION

ALL ABOUT
Australian sea lions are large marine mammals with a big head and small flippers. Males can be twice the length and weight of females. Males are usually dark brown in color. Females are silver and gray.
- **Length:** 6 to 8 feet (1.8 to 2.4 m)
- **Weight:** 550 to 660 pounds (249.5 to 299.4 kg)
- **Lifespan:** 17 to 25 years
- **Conservation Status:** Endangered

HABITAT & DIET
Australian sea lions are found along the southern coast of Australia. They prefer resting on sandy beaches. They do most of their hunting on the sea floor, dining on octopuses, sharks, rock lobsters, and cuttlefish.

FAMILY & SOCIAL LIFE
Australian sea lions live in large colonies. Females tend to stay in the area where they were born. Males travel for food and to mate. Australian sea lions have a long breeding cycle. Females are pregnant for 18 months, and pups stay with their mother for another 18 months.

DID YOU KNOW?
Australian sea lions are the only native sea lion species in Australia. They are also the rarest.

FUN FACT

Australian sea lions can hold their breath for up to 40 minutes.

BLUE WHALE

ALL ABOUT

Blue whales are the largest animals on Earth. They have baleen plates, rather than teeth, to strain water out of their mouth and keep food in.

- **Length:** 82 to 105 feet (25 to 32 m)
- **Weight:** up to 330,000 pounds (149,685.5 kg)
- **Lifespan:** 80 to 90 years
- **Conservation Status:** Endangered

HABITAT & DIET

Blue whales are found off the southern coast of Australia. They primarily dine on krill, eating up to 4 tons (3.6 mt) per day.

FUN FACT
A blue whale's tongue can weigh as much as an elephant.

FAMILY & SOCIAL LIFE

Blue whales usually swim alone or in pairs but sometimes gather in small groups. They communicate using pulses, groans, and moans that can be heard up to 1,000 miles (1,609.3 km) away.

BOTTLENOSE DOLPHIN

ALL ABOUT
Bottlenose dolphins are named for their bottle-shaped rostrums. They have a sleek gray body and a large dorsal fin that helps them swim up to 22 miles per hour (35.4 kmh).
- **Length:** 10 to 14 feet (3 to 4.3 m)
- **Weight:** 300 to 650 pounds (136.1 to 294.8 kg)
- **Lifespan:** 45 to 50 years
- **Conservation Status:** Least Concern

HABITAT & DIET
They are found all around Australia's coast, both in shallow waters close to shore and in deep ocean waters. Bottlenose dolphins are carnivores, eating a large variety of fish, shrimp, and squid.

FAMILY & SOCIAL LIFE
Bottlenose dolphins are social animals. They swim and hunt together in groups called pods.

FUN FACT
Pods of bottlenose dolphins vary in size from two to more than a thousand dolphins.

DUGONG

ALL ABOUT

Dugongs are large, brownish-gray marine mammals with a wide, flat muzzle, which is used to graze along the sea floor. Dugongs can stay underwater for up to six minutes at a time.

- **Length:** 8 to 10 feet (2.4 to 3 m)
- **Weight:** 500 to 925 pounds (226.8 to 419.6 kg)
- **Lifespan:** about 70 years
- **Conservation Status:** Vulnerable

> **DID YOU KNOW?**
> Dugongs are thought to have inspired the idea of mermaids.

HABITAT & DIET

Dugongs are found all around the northern and eastern coasts of Australia, preferring warm, shallow waters close to land. They are herbivores and only eat seagrass. Sensitive bristles on their upper lip help them find food.

FAMILY & SOCIAL LIFE

Dugongs spend much time alone or in pairs. However, large herds of as many as 100 dugongs have been spotted. Dugongs have poor eyesight, so they often communicate with one another using physical touch and sounds such as chirps, whistles, and barks.

Female dugongs give birth to one calf at a time. Calves will stay with their mother for up to 1.5 years after birth.

FUN FACT

Dugongs can eat up to 66 pounds (29.9 kg) of seagrass a day.

MAMMALS: MARINE MAMMALS

HUMPBACK WHALE

ALL ABOUT
Humpback whales are large baleen whales with a small hump in front of their dorsal fin. Their large pectoral fins can grow up to 16 feet (4.9 m) long.

- **Length:** 48 to 62.5 feet (14.6 to 19.1 m)
- **Weight:** up to 79,366 pounds (36,000 kg)
- **Lifespan:** 80 to 90 years
- **Conservation Status:** Least Concern

FUN FACT
A humpback whale's tail can be up to 18 feet (5.5 m) wide.

HABITAT & DIET

Humpback whales are usually found in open ocean waters all along the Australian coast. During their annual migration from cold to warm waters, they pass close to the coast and will stop in bays for a short time.

> **DID YOU KNOW?**
> Male humpback whales "sing" songs that can be heard 20 miles (32.2 km) away.

Humpback whales mostly eat krill, plankton, and small fish such as mackerel. They can eat up to 3,000 pounds (1,360.8 kg) of food a day.

FAMILY & SOCIAL LIFE

Humpback whales communicate with one another through moans, howls, cries, and other noises. These sounds are sometimes called whale songs. Calves have also been known to "whisper" to their mothers.

MAMMALS: MARINE MAMMALS

LEOPARD SEAL

ALL ABOUT
Leopard seals have a long, dark gray or silver body, a black-spotted coat, a large head, and a long snout. They are excellent swimmers.

- **Length:** 10 to 11.5 feet (3 to 3.5 m)
- **Weight:** 441 to 1,302 pounds (200 to 591 kg)
- **Lifespan:** 12 to 15 years
- **Conservation Status:** Least Concern

HABITAT & DIET
Leopard seals are found in Antarctic waters around the southeastern coast of Australia. They are carnivores and fierce hunters, preying on a variety of fish, squid, smaller seals, and penguins.

FAMILY & SOCIAL LIFE
Leopard seals mainly live alone, except when mating or taking care of pups. During mating season, many seals will gather in large groups on land.

FUN FACT
Female leopard seals are larger than males.

LONG-FINNED PILOT WHALE

ALL ABOUT

Long-finned pilot whales are black or dark gray with a white anchor-shaped spot on their belly. They have long flippers and a large round head.

- **Length:** 19 to 25 feet (5.8 to 7.6 m)
- **Weight:** 2,900 to 5,000 pounds (1,315.4 to 2,268 kg)
- **Lifespan:** 35 to 60 years
- **Conservation Status:** Least Concern

HABITAT & DIET

Long-finned pilot whales swim in Antarctic waters around the southern coast of Australia. They're carnivores that dine mainly on squid and octopuses.

FAMILY & SOCIAL LIFE

Long-finned pilot whales are social, often living together in multigenerational pods. There can be anywhere from 20 to 150 whales in a single pod.

FUN FACT

Long-finned pilot whales use suction, rather than grabbing, to get food into their mouth.

MELON-HEADED WHALE

ALL ABOUT

Melon-headed whales have a slim, dark gray body and a large, conical head. They usually have white markings around their mouth and dark "masks" around their eyes.

- **Length:** up to 9 feet (2.7 m)
- **Weight:** up to 496 pounds (225 kg)
- **Lifespan:** up to 45 years
- **Conservation Status:** Least Concern

FUN FACT
Melon-headed whales aren't actually whales. They're dolphins.

HABITAT & DIET

Melon-headed whales are found in deep, subtropical waters around the northern coast of Australia. Their diet consists of a variety of small fish, squid, and shrimp.

FAMILY & SOCIAL LIFE

Melon-headed whales are social, forming pods of hundreds or sometimes thousands of whales. Females stay with their pod for life, whereas males might move between groups.

MINKE WHALE

ALL ABOUT
Minke whales are dark gray with a white belly and a pointed, bullet-shaped head. Like all baleen whales, minke whales have baleen plates instead of teeth.
- **Length:** up to 35 feet (10.7 m)
- **Weight:** up to 20,000 pounds (9,071.8 kg)
- **Lifespan:** up to 50 years
- **Conservation Status:** Least Concern

HABITAT & DIET
Minke whales are found along the eastern coast, and less often the western coast, of Australia. They filter feed with their baleen, trapping krill and small fish in their mouth.

FAMILY & SOCIAL LIFE
Minke whales mostly live alone or in groups of two or three, but large groups of up to 400 have been seen. They communicate with each other through clicks, grunts, and thumps.

DID YOU KNOW?
Minke whales can stay underwater for at least 15 minutes at a time.

MAMMALS: MARINE MAMMALS

ORCA

ALL ABOUT

Orcas are sometimes called killer whales, but they are not whales. They are the largest species of dolphin. Orcas are black with distinctive white markings near their eyes and on the belly. Each orca's color pattern is unique.

FUN FACT
Orca teeth can be up to 4 inches (10.2 cm) long.

- **Length:** 23 to 32 feet (7 to 9.8 m)
- **Weight:** 3,000 to 12,000 pounds (1,360.7 to 5,443.1 kg)
- **Lifespan:** 50 to 80 years
- **Conservation Status:** Data Deficient

HABITAT & DIET

Orcas can be found in every ocean on Earth. Around Australia, they are most often seen along the southeastern coast,

inhabiting both shallow and deep waters. Orcas are carnivores, eating a broad variety of animals, including other whales, seals, penguins, otters, turtles, and fish.

FAMILY & SOCIAL LIFE

Orcas are intelligent and social animals. They travel and hunt in pods of up to 40 animals. Orcas will protect each other from danger and will help a fellow pod member who is sick or hurt.

Pods work together to hunt their prey. They have their own unique noises that its members can recognize from far away. Pods also work together to take care of their calves.

DID YOU KNOW?

Orcas sleep with only half of their brain at a time. They must always be partially awake in order to surface and breathe.

SOUTHERN RIGHT WHALE

ALL ABOUT

Southern right whales are the only large whales without dorsal fins. They are mostly black or dark gray with patches of skin called callosities.
- **Length:** 43 to 56 feet (13.1 to 17.1 m)
- **Weight:** up to 176,000 pounds (79,832.3 kg)
- **Lifespan:** up to 70 years
- **Conservation Status:** Least Concern

HABITAT & DIET

Southern right whales can be seen along Australia's southern coast. These whales skim feed. They skim the water for food, mostly plankton and krill, on or just below the surface.

DID YOU KNOW?

Whale lice and barnacles live permanently on the whales' callosities. This makes the callosities appear white in color.

FAMILY & SOCIAL LIFE

Southern right whales can live in groups of up to 12 whales, but they are more often found in groups of two or three.

SPERM WHALE

ALL ABOUT

Sperm whales have enormous heads and rounded foreheads. Their head contains an oily fluid called spermaceti, which hardens when it's cold. Scientists theorize that this helps change a whale's buoyancy, allowing it to dive deep underwater.

- **Length:** 49 to 59 feet (14.9 to 18 m)
- **Weight:** up to 110,230 pounds (50,000 kg)
- **Lifespan:** 65 to 70 years
- **Conservation Status:** Vulnerable

HABITAT & DIET

Sperm whales inhabit deep waters all around Australia but especially in the southeast. They're carnivores that primarily eat squid and octopuses.

FAMILY & SOCIAL LIFE

Female sperm whales usually travel in pods of about 15 to 20 whales, whereas males often travel alone.

DID YOU KNOW?

Sperm whales have the largest brain of any animal on Earth.

MAMMALS
ADDITIONAL MAMMALS

COMMON SPOTTED CUSCUS
- **About:** This marsupial sleeps curled in a ball on a tree branch.
- **Habitat:** rainforests, mangroves, eucalyptus forests
- **Conservation Status:** Least Concern

GHOST BAT
- **About:** Ghost bats are Australia's only carnivorous bat.
- **Habitat:** forests, savannas, shrublands, rocky areas, caves
- **Conservation Status:** Vulnerable

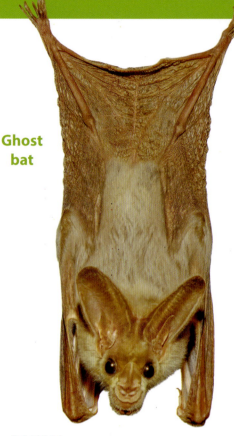
Ghost bat

Common spotted cuscus

RAKALI
- **About:** Rakali are semiaquatic and hunt for most of their food in water.
- **Habitat:** forests, wetlands
- **Conservation Status:** Least Concern

Rakali

SOUTHERN BROWN BANDICOOT
- **About:** These mammals groom themselves using their hind toes.
- **Habitat:** forests, shrublands, grasslands, wetlands
- **Conservation Status:** Least Concern

Southern brown bandicoot

WESTERN PYGMY POSSUM
- **About:** These tiny possums only grow to be about 3 inches (7.6 cm) long.
- **Habitat:** forests, shrublands
- **Conservation Status:** Least Concern

Western pygmy possum

YELLOW-FOOTED ANTECHINUS
- **About:** Male antechinus die soon after mating.
- **Habitat:** forests, savannas, shrublands, wetlands
- **Conservation Status:** Least Concern

Yellow-footed antechinus

REPTILES AND AMPHIBIANS

Reptiles are vertebrates that breathe air. They have special skin made up of scales, bony plates, or both, which they regularly shed.

Reptiles are cold-blooded. They don't maintain a constant internal body temperature. Instead, they move between sunlight and shade as needed to regulate their body temperature. During very cold weather, they may become inactive for four to five months. This time of inactivity is called brumation. During brumation, their metabolism slows down and they stop eating, although they do drink water occasionally.

Amphibians are small, cold-blooded vertebrates that need a moist environment to survive. They can breathe and absorb water through their thin skin. When they're young, most amphibians look very different from their adult forms and are aquatic. Eventually, they grow limbs and move onto land, where they spend the rest of their lives.

The eggs of reptiles and amphibians are laid in groups called clutches. For reptiles, the temperature of the environment will affect how many hatchlings will be male or female.

Red-eyed tree frogs blend in with the green trees they live in.

Sand monitors live in most of Australia.

Hawksbill turtles have a beak that allows them to reach food in hard-to-reach cracks and crevices.

REPTILES AND AMPHIBIANS
CROCODILES

FRESHWATER CROCODILE

ALL ABOUT
Freshwater crocodiles have a slender snout and large eyes that sit on top of their head. Sharp teeth protrude from their mouth. Their tough, leathery skin covers bony plates below the skin's surface.

- **Length:** 6.5 to 10 feet (2 to 3 m)
- **Weight:** up to 154 pounds (69.9 kg)
- **Lifespan:** 40 to 60 years
- **Conservation Status:** Least Concern

FUN FACT
Freshwater crocodile mothers are known to be protective of their young.

HABITAT & DIET

Freshwater crocodiles inhabit many different freshwater environments, including rivers, lagoons, and swamps, mostly in northern Australia.

> **DID YOU KNOW?**
> Freshwater crocodiles hunt using a sit-and-wait method. They lie very still in shallow water, waiting for prey to come close enough to snap up.

These reptiles are carnivorous. They eat a wide variety of insects, fish, frogs, turtles, lizards, birds, snakes, and mammals.

FAMILY & SOCIAL LIFE

During mating season, a female will dig a nest in sand near water, laying an average of 12 eggs at one time. The mother buries the eggs and returns two or three months later to dig them up after they've hatched.

SALTWATER CROCODILE

ALL ABOUT

Saltwater crocodiles are larger than freshwater crocodiles and have a broad snout. They have thick skin that ranges from golden tan to almost black in color, with bony, fixed plates that protect the animal like armor.

- **Length:** 17 to 23 feet (5.2 to 7 m)
- **Weight:** up to 330 pounds (149.7 kg)
- **Lifespan:** 40 to 70 years
- **Conservation Status:** Least Concern

FUN FACT
Saltwater crocodiles are the largest reptile in the world.

HABITAT & DIET

Saltwater crocodiles inhabit many different bodies of water in northern Australia, including rivers, estuaries, creeks, lagoons, and swamps. Contrary to their name, saltwater crocodiles can live in fresh and salt water.

Smaller crocodiles feed often, mainly eating small prey such as insects. Larger crocodiles don't eat as often but dine on bigger prey, including water birds, sea turtles, and mammals as big as water buffalo. Although smaller, younger crocodiles use the sit-and-wait hunting method, larger crocodiles will actively hunt their prey.

FAMILY & SOCIAL LIFE

Saltwater crocodiles communicate with one another using sound and visual cues such as chirping and arching their tail. Saltwater crocodiles can be aggressive with each other, especially during mating season.

DID YOU KNOW?

If prey is too large to be swallowed whole, saltwater crocodiles will tear it apart by rotating or shaking rapidly in the water.

REPTILES AND AMPHIBIANS
FROGS

CRUCIFIX FROG

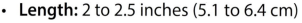

ALL ABOUT
Like all frogs, crucifix frogs are amphibians. They are bright yellow or yellowish green with a cross-shaped pattern on their back. They are burrowers, spending most of their lives underground, waiting for rain.

- **Length:** 2 to 2.5 inches (5.1 to 6.4 cm)
- **Weight:** 0.7 to 1.4 ounces (19.8 to 39.7 g)
- **Lifespan:** 6 to 8 weeks, once above ground
- **Conservation Status:** Least Concern

HABITAT & DIET
Crucifix frogs are found in grasslands and plains throughout western Australia. They dine on insects and mosquito larvae.

FAMILY & SOCIAL LIFE
Crucifix frogs lay clusters of eggs on the surface of ponds. The tadpoles stay at the bottom of the pond for about a month and a half while they grow into frogs.

FUN FACT
Crucifix frogs have webbed feet that look like spades. This shape helps the frog dig.

GREEN AND GOLDEN BELL FROG

ALL ABOUT
True to their name, green and golden bell frogs are bright green in color with gold patches.
- **Length:** up to 4 inches (10.2 cm)
- **Weight:** up to 1.8 ounces (51 g)
- **Lifespan:** 10 to 15 years
- **Conservation Status:** Near Threatened

HABITAT & DIET
Found only in a few areas around southeast Australia, these frogs live in marshes or bodies of water with grassy areas nearby. They eat a wide variety of insects, including spiders, crickets, and beetles.

FAMILY & SOCIAL LIFE
Green and golden bell frogs lay eggs in small clusters in water. The clusters sometimes attach to plants along the water's edge. Tadpoles take 3 to 11 months to grow into frogs.

FUN FACT
Green and golden bell frogs turn dark brown when they're cold.

MAGNIFICENT TREE FROG

ALL ABOUT

Magnificent tree frogs are bright green with white or yellow spots on their back. Poison glands cover their entire head to ward off predators.

- **Length:** up to 4 inches (10.2 cm)
- **Weight:** up to 3.2 ounces (90.7 g)
- **Lifespan:** about 8 years
- **Conservation Status:** Least Concern

DID YOU KNOW?

The magnificent tree frog's bright color warns predators not to eat it.

HABITAT & DIET

Magnificent tree frogs live in caves and areas of low rainfall in northwestern Australia. They eat a variety of insects, spiders, and earthworms.

FAMILY & SOCIAL LIFE

These frogs are nocturnal. Females lay an average of 1,000 eggs at one time. The tadpoles take one to four months to grow into adults.

RED-EYED TREE FROG

ALL ABOUT
Red-eyed tree frogs are bright green with a yellow belly. They have horizontal pupils and bright red or orange irises.
- **Length:** up to 2.6 inches (6.6 cm)
- **Weight:** 0.2 to 0.5 ounces (5.7 to 14.2 g)
- **Lifespan:** about 5 years
- **Conservation Status:** Least Concern

HABITAT & DIET
These nocturnal frogs are found along the eastern coast of Australia, living in tropical lowlands and forests. They dine on a variety of small insects and moths.

DID YOU KNOW?
Red-eyed tree frogs have a distinct sound. Male frogs let out a series of moans followed by a soft trill.

FAMILY & SOCIAL LIFE
Every year, a female frog lays as many as 5 clutches of up to 500 eggs each. It takes the tadpoles about 41 days to grow into frogs.

SOUTHERN CORROBOREE FROG

ALL ABOUT

Southern corroboree frogs have yellow and black stripes running along their back. Their bright colors warn predators of their poisonous skin.

Scientists believe there are between 50 and 150 of these frogs left in the wild. Southern corroboree frogs don't have any natural predators. Instead, the chytrid fungus, which causes heart disease, is their greatest threat.

- **Length:** about 1 inch (2.5 cm)
- **Weight:** up to 0.1 ounce (2.8 g)
- **Lifespan:** about 9 years
- **Conservation Status:** Critically Endangered

HABITAT & DIET

Southern corroboree frogs are only found in the Snowy Mountains of southeastern Australia. They live in bogs and swamps in mountain forests, woodlands, and heath. Southern corroboree frogs eat a wide range of beetles, insect larvae, and mites, but black ants are their favorite food.

DID YOU KNOW?

This frog's name refers to a gathering among Indigenous Australians called a "corroboree" during which they paint white stripes on their bodies.

FAMILY & SOCIAL LIFE

A female southern corroboree frog will lay a clutch of about 25 eggs in water. As the tadpoles grow, they eat algae, which helps keep the water clean for other plants and animals.

FUN FACT

Southern corroboree frogs don't hop. They walk.

TURTLE FROG

ALL ABOUT

Turtle frogs have a wide, round body, a small head, and tiny eyes. True to their name, they resemble a turtle, but without the shell. Turtle frogs range in color from light pink to dark brown. Short, muscular arms make them strong diggers.

- **Length:** up to 2 inches (5.1 cm)
- **Weight:** 0.1 to 0.3 ounces (2.8 to 8.5 g)
- **Lifespan:** up to 6 years
- **Conservation Status:** Least Concern

DID YOU KNOW?

Unlike other burrowing frogs that use their back legs, turtle frogs use their front legs to dig.

HABITAT & DIET

Turtle frogs live in underground burrows in southwestern Australia. Their only source of food is termites. One frog can eat about 400 termites in a single feeding. Turtle frogs are one of the only species of frog that can live in areas without freestanding water available.

FAMILY & SOCIAL LIFE

Unlike most frogs, turtle frogs don't have a tadpole stage. Female turtle frogs lay up to 50 eggs in a burrow. The hatchlings emerge as small but fully formed frogs.

FUN FACT
Turtle frogs can dig burrows up to 3 feet (0.9 m) deep.

REPTILES AND AMPHIBIANS
LIZARDS

AUSTRALIAN WATER DRAGON

ALL ABOUT

There are two species of Australian water dragons: the eastern water dragon and the Gippsland water dragon. Eastern water dragons are usually light greenish gray with white-and-yellow markings on their throat. Gippsland water dragons are darker grayish green with splotches of yellow, orange, or blue. All water dragons are able to change color to match their surroundings.

- **Length:** 31.5 to 35.5 inches (80 to 90.2 cm)
- **Weight:** up to 2.2 pounds (1 kg)
- **Lifespan:** up to 28 years
- **Conservation Status:** Least Concern

HABITAT & DIET

Australian water dragons are found in eastern Australia living in a wide range of habitats, from tropical rainforests to mountain streams. Water dragons are omnivores that eat a variety of plants, fruit, and insects, such as ants and cicadas.

DID YOU KNOW?

Water dragons have lived in Australia for 20 million years.

FUN FACT

Water dragons can run on just their hind legs.

FAMILY & SOCIAL LIFE

Water dragons are often found in large groups made up of one male and several females with their young. Water dragons communicate through physical movements such as head bobbing.

REPTILES AND AMPHIBIANS: LIZARDS

BARKING GECKO

ALL ABOUT
Barking geckos are named for the sound they make when threatened. They can vary in color, from light pink or purple to dark brown with spots of yellow, white, orange, or blue.

- **Length:** up to 4.5 inches (11.4 cm)
- **Weight:** 0.7 to 0.9 ounces (20 to 25 g)
- **Lifespan:** up to 15 years
- **Conservation Status:** Least Concern

HABITAT & DIET
Barking geckos can live in a wide range of habitats, including forests, heath, grasslands, shrublands, rocky hills, and dry scrublands of southern Australia. Barking geckos feed mainly on insects.

FAMILY & SOCIAL LIFE
During breeding, female barking geckos produce one to five clutches of eggs with two eggs in each clutch.

DID YOU KNOW?
The eggs can be seen through a pregnant barking gecko's stomach before she deposits them.

BEARDED DRAGON

ALL ABOUT
Bearded dragons can be a wide range of colors, from gray to orange. They have small spikes under their chin. Puffing out their chin gives the lizards the appearance of having a "beard."

- **Length:** 18 to 22 inches (45.7 to 55.9 cm)
- **Weight:** 0.6 to 1.1 pounds (0.3 to 0.5 kg)
- **Lifespan:** 4 to 10 years
- **Conservation Status:** Least Concern

HABITAT & DIET
Bearded dragons are found across almost all of Australia. They prefer warm, arid areas, such as deserts, savannas, and scrublands. These lizards are omnivores that eat insects, leaves, flowers, fruit, and occasionally small lizards or rodents.

FAMILY & SOCIAL LIFE
During mating season, a male might pound his feet, wave his arms, or bob his head to attract a female.

FUN FACT
Bearded dragons can communicate by changing the color of their beard.

BLUE-TONGUED SKINK

ALL ABOUT
Blue-tongued skinks vary in color, but all of them have a bright blue tongue, which they stick out when they feel threatened.
- **Length:** 12 to 13 inches (30.5 to 33 cm)
- **Weight:** 0.6 to 1.1 pounds (0.3 to 0.5 kg)
- **Lifespan:** 15 to 20 years
- **Conservation Status:** Least Concern

HABITAT & DIET
Blue-tongued skinks are found in woodlands and forests throughout eastern Australia. They're omnivores that dine on a variety of insects, snails, flowers, and fruit.

FAMILY & SOCIAL LIFE
Females produce eggs that hatch inside their body. The hatchlings are born live in a clutch of 10 to 15 lizards.

DID YOU KNOW?
Blue-tongued skinks don't walk on their feet. Instead, they slither on their stomach like snakes.

BOYD'S FOREST DRAGON

ALL ABOUT
Boyd's forest dragons can have bright coloring on their throat and sides. They camouflage into their surroundings to hide from predators.
- **Length:** 5.9 inches (15 cm)
- **Weight:** 3.5 to 5.3 ounces (99.2 to 150.3 g)
- **Lifespan:** up to 10 years
- **Conservation Status:** Least Concern

HABITAT & DIET
Boyd's forest dragons can be found in the rainforests of northeastern Australia. They spend most of their time in trees. These lizards are omnivores that dine on small insects and worms and sometimes fruit and flowers.

> **DID YOU KNOW?**
> Boyd's forest dragons don't sunbathe like most lizards. They allow their body temperature to change with the conditions surrounding them.

FAMILY & SOCIAL LIFE
Females lay one to six eggs in a nest on the forest floor. The eggs remain there for up to the three months before they hatch.

CENTRAL NETTED DRAGON

ALL ABOUT
Central netted dragons are named for the black, netlike pattern on their skin. It helps them camouflage. Their strong legs and toes allow them to run fast and burrow.

- **Length:** 4 inches (10.2 cm)
- **Weight:** 0.5 to 0.9 ounces (14.2 to 25 g)
- **Lifespan:** 2 to 4 years
- **Conservation Status:** Least Concern

HABITAT & DIET
Central netted dragons are found throughout western and central Australia, preferring grasslands, shrublands, and desert plains. These lizards are omnivores that mostly eat insects, leaves, and flowers.

FAMILY & SOCIAL LIFE
They are active during the day and spend a lot of time basking in the sun.

DID YOU KNOW?
Central netted dragons usually have six to eight burrows around their home range that are used to escape predators and keep cool.

CUNNINGHAM'S SKINK

ALL ABOUT

Cunningham's skinks are reddish brown to black with a long, spiny tail. They were named after the explorer and botanist Alan Cunningham, who collected the first specimen.

- **Length:** 9.8 to 11.8 inches (24.9 to 30 cm)
- **Weight:** 0.5 to 0.6 pounds (0.2 to 0.3 kg)
- **Lifespan:** 20 to 30 years
- **Conservation Status:** Least Concern

DID YOU KNOW?

When threatened, Cunningham's skinks get into a rock crevice and puff up their body, wedging themselves between the rocks.

HABITAT & DIET

Cunningham's skinks are found in forests and woodlands in southeastern Australia, often basking on rocks. They're omnivores that eat an assortment of insects, slugs, and snails, as well as fruit and leaves.

FAMILY & SOCIAL LIFE

Cunningham's skinks live in large groups. Unlike many reptiles, young Cunningham's skinks stay with their mother for a while after hatching.

FRILLED LIZARD

ALL ABOUT

Frilled lizards are gray to brown in color. When threatened, they open their mouth wide, causing their frill of skin around their neck to open. The frill can be as wide as 12 inches (30.5 cm) and yellow, orange, and brown in color. This makes the lizards look larger to predators.

- **Length:** 27 to 37 inches (68.6 to 94 cm)
- **Weight:** 1 to 2.2 pounds (0.5 to 1 kg)
- **Lifespan:** 10 to 20 years
- **Conservation Status:** Least Concern

HABITAT & DIET

Frilled lizards are found in the tropical forests and savanna woodlands of northern Australia. They spend most of their time in trees but descend to eat. They dine on an assortment of ants, spiders, cicadas, termites, and small lizards and mammals.

FAMILY & SOCIAL LIFE

Frilled lizards live alone except when breeding. During mating season, female frilled lizards lay between 8 and 23 eggs in an underground nest. The eggs incubate for about 70 days before they hatch. Hatchlings are not cared for by a parent and are fully independent.

DID YOU KNOW?

If a predator isn't intimidated by the lizard's frill, the lizard will turn and run on its hind legs.

FUN FACT

The frill also helps regulate the lizard's body temperature.

LACE MONITOR

ALL ABOUT

Lace monitors are large lizards with a long tail. They are usually dark gray and black with bands of yellowish skin across their back.

- **Length:** 5 to 6.5 feet (1.5 to 2 m)
- **Weight:** up to 30 pounds (13.6 kg)
- **Lifespan:** 10 to 15 years
- **Conservation Status:** Least Concern

HABITAT & DIET

Lace monitors are found in forests throughout eastern Australia. They spend most of their time in trees. They are carnivorous and eat a diet of possums, rabbits, wallabies, insects, and eggs.

FAMILY & SOCIAL LIFE

A female monitor will burrow into a termite mound and lay eggs inside. The termites repair the hole, which allows the eggs to incubate.

DID YOU KNOW?

Lace monitor teeth curve backward, making it hard for prey to escape.

PAINTED DRAGON

ALL ABOUT
Painted dragons have colors that can vary from gray or brown to orange. Males have bright blue along their sides and can have a yellow head and throat.
- **Length:** up to 8 inches (20.3 cm)
- **Weight:** not enough data
- **Lifespan:** 2 to 4 years
- **Conservation Status:** Least Concern

DID YOU KNOW?
A row of comblike scales beneath their eyes gives painted dragons the scientific name *Ctenophorus*, which means "comb-bearer."

HABITAT & DIET
Painted dragons live in a range of dry habitats, including savannas, grasslands, and sand dunes, in central and southern Australia. They are carnivores that dine on a range of insects.

FAMILY & SOCIAL LIFE
During breeding season, males twist and bob their head to attract females. Female dragons usually lay one clutch of four eggs each breeding season.

PERENTIE

ALL ABOUT

Perenties are the largest lizard species in Australia. They have a long body and tail, a forked tongue, and sharp teeth. They're usually brown, speckled with dark spots, and have large white or pale-yellow bands across their back and tail.

Perenties can expand and contract the sides of their neck. This pumps air into the lungs, allowing perenties to run fast.

- **Length:** 6.5 to 8 feet (2 to 2.4 m)
- **Weight:** up to 33 pounds (15 kg)
- **Lifespan:** 15 to 20 years
- **Conservation Status:** Least Concern

FUN FACT
Perenties usually swallow their meal whole.

HABITAT & DIET

Perenties are found throughout central Australia, preferring arid regions. Perenties are carnivores that eat a wide variety of meat, including insects, birds, reptiles, and fish. They can hunt prey as large as wombats or small kangaroos.

DID YOU KNOW?

Perenties are rarely encountered by people in the wild because they're shy and live in remote areas.

FAMILY & SOCIAL LIFE

During mating season, a male perentie courts a female by licking or nuzzling her. After mating, the female lays a clutch of 6 to 12 eggs, usually in a termite mound. The eggs take about 220 days to hatch.

SHINGLEBACK LIZARD

ALL ABOUT
Singleback lizards have a short, fat tail and a dark blue tongue. They are covered in large, dark brown scales.
- **Length:** 10 to 12 inches (25.4 to 30.5 cm)
- **Weight:** up to 2.4 pounds (1.1 kg)
- **Lifespan:** 15 to 20 years
- **Conservation Status:** Least Concern

DID YOU KNOW?
To scare off predators, a shingleback lizard opens its mouth wide and sticks out its blue tongue.

HABITAT & DIET
Found across southern Australia, shingleback lizards prefer semiarid plains and woodlands with grass and leaf litter to shelter under. As omnivores, they eat plants and slow-moving animals, such as snails and beetles.

FAMILY & SOCIAL LIFE
Shingleback lizards mostly live alone, except when breeding. Unlike most lizards, female shinglebacks give birth to live young. Females often have one to three babies at a time.

SOUTHERN LEAF-TAILED GECKO

ALL ABOUT
Southern leaf-tailed geckos are named after their leaf-shaped tail, which is wide at the base and narrow at the end. These geckos have rough, scaly skin that ranges from light to dark brown in color.

> **DID YOU KNOW?**
> A smooth tail on a southern leaf-tailed gecko indicates that the tail has recently been regrown.

- **Length:** up to 4 inches (10.2 cm)
- **Weight:** 0.4 to 1.1 ounces (11.3 to 30 g)
- **Lifespan:** about 8 years
- **Conservation Status:** Least Concern

HABITAT & DIET
Southern leaf-tailed geckos are only found in a small area of southeast Australia called the Sydney Basin. They live in coastal sandstone heath. These carnivores eat various insects, spiders, and moths.

FAMILY & SOCIAL LIFE
Each year, females lay two to three clutches of eggs in rock or log crevices.

THORNY DEVIL

ALL ABOUT
Named for the thornlike spikes all over their body, thorny devils are usually light brown or gray in color with dark brown or golden patches that help them camouflage. A large bump on their neck serves as a fake head to warn off predators.

Thorny devils have a distinct walk that consists of slow, jerky movements. They scoot backward and forward as they go, which is thought to be a defense mechanism to confuse predators.

- **Length:** 3 to 4.5 inches (7.6 to 11.4 cm)
- **Weight:** 1.2 to 3.1 ounces (34 to 88 g)
- **Lifespan:** 6 years
- **Conservation Status:** Least Concern

HABITAT & DIET
Thorny devils are found throughout most arid regions of western and central Australia.

FUN FACT
Thorny devils change color depending on the temperature.

The thorny devil's diet consists entirely of ants. A thorny devil can consume more than a thousand ants daily.

FAMILY & SOCIAL LIFE

During mating season, a male thorny devil bobs his head and waves his legs to attract a mate. The female lays between 3 and 10 eggs in an underground burrow about 1 foot (0.3 m) deep. The eggs take three to four months to hatch.

> **DID YOU KNOW?**
>
> At the base of each thornlike spike is a groove that collects water. The grooves funnel water toward the lizard's mouth.

REPTILES AND AMPHIBIANS
RIVER TURTLES

PIG-NOSED TURTLE

ALL ABOUT
With a snout like a pig's, the pig-nosed turtle has a gray body, flipper-shaped front limbs, and webbed hind legs.
- **Length:** up to 27.5 inches (69.9 cm)
- **Weight:** up to 35.3 pounds (16 kg)
- **Lifespan:** up to 38 years (under human care)
- **Conservation Status:** Endangered

HABITAT & DIET
Pig-nosed turtles live in tropical rivers, streams, lakes, and lagoons in a small part of northern Australia. They are omnivores that mainly eat plant matter, fruit, and nuts. They will also eat snails, insects, shrimp, and small fish.

FAMILY & SOCIAL LIFE
Pig-nosed turtles spend most of their time in water, usually only leaving to nest.

FUN FACT
Females communicate with each other to find nesting sites on land.

RED-BELLIED SHORT-NECKED TURTLE

ALL ABOUT

Red-bellied short-necked turtles are also known as pink-bellied side-necked turtles, as their belly is often red or pink. Their shells can range in color from tan to dark brown or gray.

DID YOU KNOW?

These turtles communicate with one another using a wide range of sounds that are too quiet for humans to hear.

- **Length:** 5 to 10 inches (12.7 to 25.4 cm)
- **Weight:** up to 49.5 pounds (22.5 kg)
- **Lifespan:** 15 to 20 years (under human care)
- **Conservation Status:** Least Concern

HABITAT & DIET

In Australia, these turtles are only found in and around the Jardine River. They prefer slow-moving bodies of water. As omnivores, red-bellied short-necked turtles eat algae, fish, insects, and mollusks.

FAMILY & SOCIAL LIFE

Female red-bellied short-necked turtles deposit their eggs in a hole they leave uncovered. Once the eggs are laid, the mother abandons them.

SNAKE-NECKED TURTLE

ALL ABOUT
Snake-necked turtles, also known as long-necked turtles, have a long, thin neck. Their light brown or black shell is broad, flat, and oval shaped. They have claws and webbed feet.
- **Length:** up to 11 inches (27.9 cm)
- **Weight:** up to 1.8 pounds (0.8 kg)
- **Lifespan:** 31 to 37 years
- **Conservation Status:** Not Assessed

HABITAT & DIET
Snake-necked turtles are found in southeastern Australia in rivers and streams, but they most commonly live in slow-moving waters such as swamps or wetlands. Snake-necked turtles are semiaquatic, spending time both in water and on land.

Snake-necked turtles are carnivores. They eat fish, plankton, and aquatic insects. They catch their prey by opening their mouth and rapidly lowering their hyoid bone in their neck. This creates a vacuum, which sucks prey into their mouth.

FAMILY & SOCIAL LIFE
Snake-necked turtles mostly live alone, except during mating season. Females dig nests near water and lay between 8 and 24 eggs per year.

FUN FACT
These turtles bend their head sideways into their shell instead of directly back.

DID YOU KNOW?

When their habitats become too hot or dry, snake-necked turtles will burrow under fallen leaves and estivate, or become dormant.

REPTILES AND AMPHIBIANS
SEA TURTLES

FLATBACK SEA TURTLE

ALL ABOUT
Flatback sea turtles get their name from their flat shells, which are olive gray with tan or yellow along the edges.
- **Length:** 2.5 to 3 feet (0.8 to 0.9 m)
- **Weight:** up to 220 pounds (100 kg)
- **Lifespan:** about 50 years
- **Conservation Status:** Data Deficient

FUN FACT
Flatback turtle eggs are about the size of billiard balls.

HABITAT & DIET
In Australia, flatback sea turtles are only found on the northern coast. They prefer to live in bays, coral reefs, and shallow, grassy waters. They are omnivores, dining on seaweed, sea cucumbers, jellyfish, prawns, and other small sea creatures.

FAMILY & SOCIAL LIFE
Female flatback turtles lay two or three clutches of 50 to 70 eggs each. When they're born, the hatchlings are larger than the hatchlings of most turtle species.

GREEN SEA TURTLE

ALL ABOUT
Although its shell is brown or olive, a green sea turtle's body is green, which might be due to its plant-based diet.
- **Length:** up to 5 feet (1.5 m)
- **Weight:** 250 to 400 pounds (113.4 to 181.4 kg)
- **Lifespan:** at least 70 years
- **Conservation Status:** Endangered

FUN FACT
Green sea turtles are one of the largest hard-shelled sea turtles, weighing up to 700 pounds (317.5 kg).

HABITAT & DIET
Green sea turtles are found in almost every ocean in the world. The Australian coast has one of the largest nesting populations. Unlike most sea turtles, green sea turtles are mainly herbivores. Their diet consists of seaweed and seagrass.

FAMILY & SOCIAL LIFE
Green sea turtles spend most of their time underwater, but female turtles will leave the ocean to lay eggs on the beach.

HAWKSBILL TURTLE

ALL ABOUT
Hawksbill turtles get their name from their mouth, which resembles a hawk's beak. Their shell can be many colors, including amber, orange, brown, yellow, red, and black.
- **Length:** 2 to 3.5 feet (0.6 to 1.1 m)
- **Weight:** 100 to 150 pounds (45.4 to 68 kg)
- **Lifespan:** 30 to 50 years
- **Conservation Status:** Critically Endangered

HABITAT & DIET
Hawksbill turtles are found in tropical waters around northern Australia, where they tend to stay close to the coastline. They are omnivores that eat algae as well as mollusks, sea urchins, jellyfish, and other marine life.

FAMILY & SOCIAL LIFE
Female hawksbill turtles return to a beach in the same area where they were born to nest every two to five years. They lay between 130 and 160 eggs at a time.

FUN FACT
When hawksbill turtles are young, their shell is heart shaped.

LEATHERBACK TURTLE

ALL ABOUT
Leatherback turtles have a soft, leathery shell—hence the name. Their shells are black with white or yellow spots.
- **Length:** up to 7 feet (2.1 m)
- **Weight:** 750 to 1,000 pounds (340.2 to 453.6 kg)
- **Lifespan:** 45 to 50 years
- **Conservation Status:** Vulnerable

FUN FACT
Leatherback turtles are the largest turtles on Earth and can weigh up to 1,000 pounds (453.6 kg).

HABITAT & DIET
Leatherback turtles are found around the entire Australian coast, including the Great Barrier Reef. Their diet consists mainly of soft-bodied sea creatures such as jellyfish and salps, a type of marine animal also called a sea squirt.

FAMILY & SOCIAL LIFE
Leatherback turtles spend almost their entire life in the ocean. Only female turtles leave the water to dig nests for their eggs, laying about 100 at a time.

LOGGERHEAD SEA TURTLE

ALL ABOUT

Loggerhead sea turtles have a reddish-brown shell, neck, and flippers. They get their name from their large heads.
- **Length:** 2.5 to 3.5 feet (0.8 to 1.1 m)
- **Weight:** 200 to 350 pounds (90.7 to 158.8 kg)
- **Lifespan:** 70 years or more
- **Conservation Status:** Vulnerable

HABITAT & DIET

Loggerhead turtles are found in nearly every ocean on Earth. They live all around the Australian coast and along the Great Barrier Reef. They're carnivores that eat hard-shelled creatures such as crabs and soft sea creatures such as jellyfish.

FAMILY & SOCIAL LIFE

Loggerhead turtles are excellent navigators, migrating thousands of miles throughout their life. Females usually return to a beach in the same area where they were born to lay their own eggs.

FUN FACT

Loggerhead turtles have powerful jaws designed to crush the shells of their prey.

REPTILES AND AMPHIBIANS: SEA TURTLES

OLIVE RIDLEY TURTLE

ALL ABOUT
Olive ridley turtles are the smallest sea turtle species. Their name comes from the olive green color of their skin and shell.
- **Length:** 2 to 2.5 feet (0.6 to 0.8 m)
- **Weight:** up to 100 pounds (45.4 kg)
- **Lifespan:** 30 to 50 years
- **Conservation Status:** Vulnerable

DID YOU KNOW?
Olive ridley turtles can dive up to 500 feet (152.4 m) to eat animals along the ocean floor.

HABITAT & DIET
Olive ridley turtles are mainly found in the open ocean but can also be found around the northern coast of Australia. They are omnivores and eat a variety of algae, lobsters, crabs, and mollusks.

FAMILY & SOCIAL LIFE
Olive ridley turtles come ashore in large numbers. Sometimes hundreds of thousands gather on beaches to nest at the same time. This is known as arribada nesting.

REPTILES AND AMPHIBIANS
SNAKES

AUSTRALIAN SCRUB PYTHON

ALL ABOUT
The largest snake in Australia is the scrub python. It has smooth, dark yellow or golden scales with black bands that form a netlike pattern. This snake is also known as the amethystine python, due to its scales' resemblance to amethyst quartz.

- **Length:** 16 to 26 feet (4.9 to 7.9 m)
- **Weight:** up to 55.1 pounds (25 kg)
- **Lifespan:** 20 to 30 years
- **Conservation Status:** Least Concern

FUN FACT
Scrub pythons have flexible jaws that help them swallow large prey whole.

HABITAT & DIET
Scrub pythons are found in tropical areas in northeastern Australia, living in forests, savanna woodlands, vine thickets, scrub, and rainforests. The young spend most of their time in trees but move to the ground when they're older.

Scrub pythons are nocturnal hunters, eating a wide variety of prey, including rodents, birds, lizards, wild pigs, wallabies, and young kangaroos. They first catch prey with their teeth before squeezing it to death.

FAMILY & SOCIAL LIFE

Female scrub pythons lay a clutch of between 5 and 21 eggs, which take 80 to 90 days to incubate. During this time, the mother coils around the eggs, protecting them from predators.

DID YOU KNOW?

Scrub pythons use heat-sensing pits on the front of their head to detect prey at night.

BANDY-BANDY SNAKE

DID YOU KNOW?
The bandy-bandy snake scares off predators by rising and creating loops with its body in the air to make itself look bigger.

ALL ABOUT
The bandy-bandy snake is small with a black head and black-and-white rings down its body.

- **Length:** 15.4 to 23.6 inches (39.1 to 59.9 cm)
- **Weight:** not enough data
- **Lifespan:** unknown
- **Conservation Status:** Least Concern

HABITAT & DIET
Bandy-bandy snakes are found throughout northeastern Australia in a wide range of habitats, including coastal forests, woodlands, scrublands, mulga, and deserts. They primarily eat a group of small snakes called blind snakes.

FAMILY & SOCIAL LIFE
Bandy-bandy snakes are nocturnal and spend most of their time in underground burrows. They tend to hunt for food right after it has rained.

BLACK-HEADED PYTHON

ALL ABOUT
Black-headed pythons have a black head and brown or yellow scales with wavy black stripes down its body.
- **Length:** 7 to 9 feet (2.1 to 2.7 m)
- **Weight:** 6.6 to 15.4 pounds (3 to 7 kg)
- **Lifespan:** 20 to 30 years
- **Conservation Status:** Least Concern

HABITAT & DIET
Black-headed pythons live in woodlands, rainforests, or semiarid regions of northeastern Australia. They're carnivores that dine on small rodents, lizards, and frogs.

FAMILY & SOCIAL LIFE
Black-headed pythons most commonly live alone, except when breeding or taking care of hatchlings. Female pythons lay a clutch of 8 to 18 eggs at a time and coil around them for about two months before they hatch.

DID YOU KNOW?
Although black-headed pythons are nonvenomous, they are resistant to other snakes' venom and can eat venomous snakes as well.

COMMON DEATH ADDER

ALL ABOUT
Common death adders are dark red to grayish brown in color, with a flat, triangular head. They are nocturnal.
- **Length:** 16 to 39 inches (40.6 to 99 cm)
- **Weight:** up to 2.2 pounds (1 kg)
- **Lifespan:** up to 15 years
- **Conservation Status:** Least Concern

HABITAT & DIET
Common death adders normally live in forests, woodlands, grasslands, or heath around the eastern and southern regions of Australia. They eat frogs, lizards, birds, and sometimes small mammals.

DID YOU KNOW?
The tip of a common death adder's tail looks like a small grub, which the snake uses to lure prey.

FAMILY & SOCIAL LIFE
Common death adders spend most of their time alone, except when breeding. Unlike most snakes, death adders give birth to live young.

EASTERN BROWN SNAKE

ALL ABOUT
Eastern brown snakes are one of the world's most venomous snakes. True to their name, these snakes can be almost any shade of brown.
- **Length:** up to 7 feet (2.1 m)
- **Weight:** about 5.5 pounds (2.5 kg)
- **Lifespan:** unknown
- **Conservation Status:** Least Concern

DID YOU KNOW?
Because they can swallow large prey, eastern brown snakes may only need to eat a few meals a year.

HABITAT & DIET
Eastern brown snakes are found all over eastern Australia in a wide range of habitats, including woodlands, scrublands, and savanna grasslands. They eat a variety of animals, including frogs, reptiles, birds, and mice.

FAMILY & SOCIAL LIFE
During breeding season, male eastern brown snakes fight each other for a mate by wrestling and forcing the other's head to the ground.

GREEN TREE PYTHON

ALL ABOUT

Green tree pythons are named for their vibrant green color. They can have stripes or spots of white, yellow, green, or blue.

To hunt, green tree pythons drape themselves over a branch in a series of loops with their head hanging down, ready to strike when prey comes near.

These snakes have heat-sensing pits near their nose that help them find warm-blooded prey, even at night. Instead of using venom, green tree pythons kill their prey by squeezing it.

- **Length:** 4 to 7 feet (1.2 to 2.1 m)
- **Weight:** up to 3.5 pounds (1.6 kg)
- **Lifespan:** 10 to 20 years
- **Conservation Status:** Least Concern

HABITAT & DIET

Green tree pythons are found in the rainforest on the Cape York Peninsula in northeastern Australia. As hatchlings, they consume insects, whereas adults eat a variety of lizards, birds, and small mammals such as mice.

DID YOU KNOW?

Green tree pythons can open their jaws 180 degrees wide, allowing them to eat prey that is up to three times larger than their head.

FUN FACT
Hatchlings can be red or yellow when they're born.

FAMILY & SOCIAL LIFE
During mating season, a female green tree python lays a clutch of 10 to 30 eggs. She wraps herself around the eggs while they incubate for about 50 days. Once hatched, the young fend for themselves.

INLAND TAIPAN

ALL ABOUT
Inland taipans vary from light to dark brown with a yellow belly. But these snakes change color with the seasons, becoming darker during the winter and lighter in the summer.
- **Length:** up to 8.2 feet (2.5 m)
- **Weight:** 2.2 to 4.4 pounds (1 to 2 kg)
- **Lifespan:** 10 to 15 years (under human care)
- **Conservation Status:** Least Concern

HABITAT & DIET
Inland taipans are found in the hot, dry climate of Australia's eastern interior, seeking deep cracks in the ground as refuge. Inland taipans feast on small mammals such as mice and rats.

DID YOU KNOW?
This snake has the most toxic venom of any land snake in the world. A single bite has enough venom to kill 100 adult men.

FAMILY & SOCIAL LIFE
Female inland taipans lay clutches of up to 20 eggs. After laying the eggs, the mother abandons them.

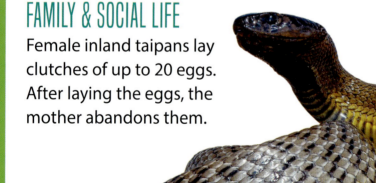

LOWLAND COPPERHEAD

ALL ABOUT
The lowland copperhead snake gets its name from the coppery scales along its sides.
- **Length:** 2.5 to 5 feet (0.8 to 1.5 m)
- **Weight:** not enough data
- **Lifespan:** about 18 years
- **Conservation Status:** Least Concern

HABITAT & DIET
Lowland copperheads are found in southeast Australia. They prefer cold, wet climates and live in grasslands, heath, woodlands, and open scrub. These snakes mainly eat insects, frogs, lizards, and other snakes.

FAMILY & SOCIAL LIFE
Lowland copperheads are most active during the day, spending much of their time on the ground. They sometimes climb trees to reach sunlight.

FUN FACT
Lowland copperheads are ovoviviparous, which means eggs hatch inside the female's body.

MULGA SNAKE

ALL ABOUT
Also known as a king brown snake, a mulga's coloring varies depending on its habitat. This adaptation helps it blend into its environment.
- **Length:** 8 to 10 feet (2.4 to 3 m)
- **Weight:** 6.6 to 8.8 pounds (3 to 4 kg)
- **Lifespan:** up to 25 years (under human care)
- **Conservation Status:** Least Concern

DID YOU KNOW?
Mulga snakes are named after mulga, a type of shrub these snakes like to live near.

HABITAT & DIET
Mulga snakes are found throughout all of Australia, except in the southeast. They live in a wide range of habitats including woodlands, grasslands, scrublands, and deserts. They dine on frogs, reptiles, birds, and small mammals.

FAMILY & SOCIAL LIFE
Mulga snakes are active during the day and at night. Their breeding season varies depending on where they live.

RED-BELLIED BLACK SNAKE

ALL ABOUT
Red-bellied black snakes are named for the red scales along their belly. They are one of the most commonly encountered snakes in Australia.
- **Length:** 5 to 6.6 feet (1.5 to 2 m)
- **Weight:** 2.2 to 4.4 pounds (1 to 2 kg)
- **Lifespan:** up to 12 years
- **Conservation Status:** Least Concern

FUN FACT
These snakes can stay underwater for up to 23 minutes at a time.

HABITAT & DIET
Found throughout eastern Australia, red-bellied black snakes prefer wet habitats such as swamps and lagoons in forests, woodlands, and grasslands. These snakes are carnivores that eat fish, tadpoles, frogs, lizards, and mammals.

FAMILY & SOCIAL LIFE
Female red-bellied black snakes give birth to live young. Pregnant females have been known to share nests at night, possibly to protect against predators.

SMALL-EYED SNAKE

ALL ABOUT

Small-eyed snakes have glossy, bluish-black scales and a white or coral pink belly. During the day, they often shelter beneath rocks or fallen trees.
- **Length:** up to 3 feet (0.9 m)
- **Weight:** not enough data
- **Lifespan:** unknown
- **Conservation Status:** Least Concern

HABITAT & DIET

Small-eyed snakes are found in eastern Australia, preferring moist habitats, such as rainforests. Small-eyed snakes are carnivores that mainly eat other reptiles.

DID YOU KNOW?

The amount of poison in the small-eyed snake's venom varies depending on where it lives.

FAMILY & SOCIAL LIFE

During the winter, small-eyed snakes are known to gather in groups of up to 29 individuals and shelter together. Female snakes are ovoviviparous and give birth to up to eight live young at a time.

TIGER SNAKE

ALL ABOUT

Tiger snakes are one of the world's deadliest snakes. They get their name from the yellow-and-black stripes that many have along their body.

> **DID YOU KNOW?**
>
> Tiger snakes are good climbers and have been found as high as 33 feet (10.1 m) above the ground.

- **Length:** 3.3 to 6.6 feet (1 to 2 m)
- **Weight:** 2.2 to 4.4 pounds (1 to 2 kg)
- **Lifespan:** 10 to 15 years
- **Conservation Status:** Least Concern

HABITAT & DIET

Tiger snakes are found throughout southern Australia, especially the southeast. They live in watery habitats, such as creeks, lagoons, wetlands, and swamps. Tiger snakes are carnivores. They eat a wide range of animals, including fish, frogs, lizards, birds, and mammals.

FAMILY & SOCIAL LIFE

Tiger snakes are most active during the day. Because of their venom and aggressive nature, they can be very dangerous.

YELLOW-BELLIED SEA SNAKE

ALL ABOUT
Yellow-bellied sea snakes can live their entire lives in the water without ever coming onto land. They have a paddle-like tail that helps them move through the water.
- **Length:** up to 3 feet long (0.9 m)
- **Weight:** 3.2 to 8.5 ounces (90.7 to 241 g)
- **Lifespan:** 2 to 4 years
- **Conservation Status:** Least Concern

HABITAT & DIET
Yellow-bellied sea snakes live in the ocean along the southeastern coast of Australia. These snakes only eat fish.

FAMILY & SOCIAL LIFE
In open waters, yellow-bellied sea snakes can be found in large numbers near lines of ocean debris such as foam or scum.

FUN FACT
Yellow-bellied sea snakes can spend up to 3.5 hours underwater between breaths.

YELLOW-FACED WHIP SNAKE

ALL ABOUT
Yellow-faced whip snakes are pale gray to brown in color with a gray-green or yellowish belly.
- **Length:** 31.5 to 39 inches (80 to 99 cm)
- **Weight:** not enough data
- **Lifespan:** unknown
- **Conservation Status:** Least Concern

DID YOU KNOW?
Despite the name, a yellow-faced whip snake's face is not always yellow.

HABITAT & DIET
Yellow-faced whip snakes are found throughout Australia but are especially common in the east. They can live in a wide range of habitats, including coastal forests, scrublands, and grasslands. They mainly eat small lizards, lizard eggs, and frogs.

FAMILY & SOCIAL LIFE
Yellow-faced whip snakes are often found in pairs or groups. Multiple female snakes might lay their eggs in one nest. Nests of up to 200 eggs have been found.

REPTILES AND AMPHIBIANS
ADDITIONAL REPTILES & AMPHIBIANS

CANE TOAD

- **About:** These toads produce a milky poison.
- **Habitat:** forests, savannas, grasslands, wetlands
- **Conservation Status:** Least Concern

Cane toad

Coastal taipan

COASTAL TAIPAN

- **About:** These snakes are one of the most venomous snake species in the world.
- **Habitat:** forests, shrublands
- **Conservation Status:** Least Concern

DIAMOND PYTHON

- **About:** These pythons are named for the diamond pattern on their back.
- **Habitat:** forests, savannas, shrublands, grasslands, wetlands
- **Conservation Status:** Least Concern

Diamond python

Gidgee skink

Pobblebonk

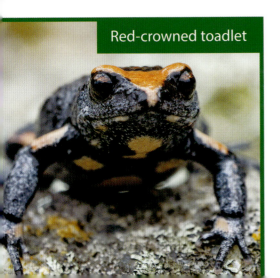
Red-crowned toadlet

GIDGEE SKINK
- **About:** These skinks can inhale air to wedge themselves in a crevice, preventing a predator from pulling them out.
- **Habitat:** shrublands, grasslands, rocky areas
- **Conservation Status:** Least Concern

POBBLEBONK
- **About:** Pobblebonks use their hind legs to dig backward into the ground.
- **Habitat:** forests, savannas, shrublands, grasslands, wetlands
- **Conservation Status:** Least Concern

RED-CROWNED TOADLET
- **About:** These frogs get their name for the red coloring on their head.
- **Habitat:** forests, shrublands, wetlands, rocky areas
- **Conservation Status:** Near Threatened

BIRDS

All birds are vertebrates and have wings. Although most birds can fly, some species have evolved to be flightless. For the majority of birds, however, nearly everything about their anatomy helps them fly. The front edge of their wings is thicker than the back edge, and they are covered with feathers that narrow to a point. This wing shape helps create lift necessary for flying. Tail feathers are used to steer while in flight.

In addition, birds have hollow bones. The hollow spaces allow oxygen to flow through their body, providing increased energy for flying.

Reproduction is also influenced by their ability to fly. Instead of carrying their babies inside their bodies, which would make them heavy, birds lay eggs. Birds then incubate the eggs in a nest for a period of time.

Female black swans are smaller than males.

Budgerigars can have up to 3,000 feathers.

AUSTRALIAN BUSTARD

ALL ABOUT

The Australian bustard is one of the largest birds in Australia. It is mostly gray and brown in color and sometimes has a black crown. Australian bustards walk with their head and neck held high.

- **Height:** 31.5 to 47 inches (80 to 119.4 cm)
- **Weight:** 9.5 to 28.2 pounds (4.3 to 12.8 kg)
- **Lifespan:** up to 25 years
- **Conservation Status:** Least Concern

HABITAT & DIET

Australian bustards inhabit dry plains, grasslands, and open woodlands all around Australia. As omnivores, they eat a variety of leaves, buds, seeds, fruit, and small animals such as frogs and lizards.

FAMILY & SOCIAL LIFE

During mating season, male bustards puff up their throat and make a deep roaring sound to attract females.

FUN FACT

The Australian bustard is Australia's heaviest flying bird.

AUSTRALIAN KING PARROT

ALL ABOUT

The Australian king parrot is mostly red and green, but it can have patches of blue-and-yellow feathers.

- **Height:** 16 to 17 inches (40.6 to 43.2 cm)
- **Weight:** 6.8 to 9.6 ounces (192.8 to 272.2 g)
- **Lifespan:** about 25 years
- **Conservation Status:** Least Concern

HABITAT & DIET

Australian king parrots are found in eastern Australia. They live in rainforests or wet sclerophyll forests, where they search for seeds, fruit, and insects.

FUN FACT

Male king parrots have a red head, whereas females have a green head.

FAMILY & SOCIAL LIFE

During breeding season, female Australian king parrots lay their eggs at the bottom of a hollow tree trunk. The entrance to the tree nest can sometimes be 33 feet (10.1 m) high, which protects the eggs from predators and heat.

AUSTRALIAN RINGNECK

ALL ABOUT

The size and color of Australian ringnecks vary, but all are mostly green with a band of yellow feathers around their neck.

- **Height:** 12 to 17 inches (30.5 to 43.2 cm)
- **Weight:** 4.3 to 7.2 ounces (121.9 to 204.1 g)
- **Lifespan:** up to 18 years (under human care)
- **Conservation Status:** Least Concern

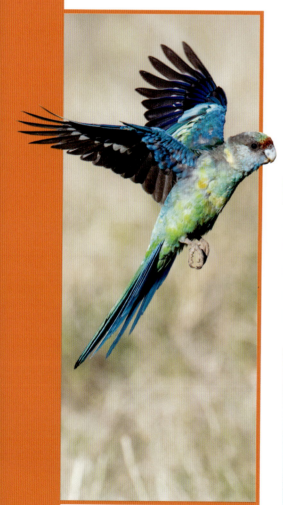

HABITAT & DIET

These birds live only in Australia. Their habitats range from arid regions to coastal areas. Their diet consists of seeds, fruit, flowers, nectar, and insects.

FAMILY & SOCIAL LIFE

Australian ringnecks lay their eggs in the holes of trees. While the mother incubates the eggs, the male feeds her. When the babies hatch, both parents feed them.

DID YOU KNOW?

In Western Australia, these birds are known as twenty-eights because one of their calls sounds like they are saying "twenty-eight."

BARKING OWL

ALL ABOUT
The barking owl is a gray-and-brown bird with white spots and bright yellow eyes.

- **Height:** 14 to 18 inches (35.6 to 45.7 cm)
- **Weight:** 0.8 to 1.4 pounds (0.4 to 0.6 kg)
- **Lifespan:** up to 20 years
- **Conservation Status:** Least Concern

HABITAT & DIET
Barking owls are found along the north and west coasts and eastern region of Australia. They most commonly live in savanna woodlands. As carnivores, they dine on a variety of birds, reptiles, insects, and small- to medium-sized mammals.

FAMILY & SOCIAL LIFE
Barking owls are crepuscular, meaning they are active at twilight. They make their nests in the hole of a live tree trunk.

FUN FACT
Barking owls have two distinct calls. One sounds like a human's scream, and the other sounds like a dog's bark.

BLACK SWAN

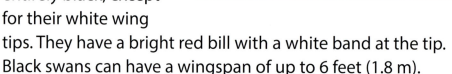

ALL ABOUT
Black swans are almost entirely black, except for their white wing tips. They have a bright red bill with a white band at the tip. Black swans can have a wingspan of up to 6 feet (1.8 m).
- **Height:** 3.5 to 5 feet (1.1 to 1.5 m)
- **Weight:** up to 20 pounds (9.1 kg)
- **Lifespan:** 10 to 15 years
- **Conservation Status:** Least Concern

DID YOU KNOW?
A black swan's neck has 25 vertebrae in it, which makes it very flexible.

HABITAT & DIET
Black swans are found throughout Australia. During breeding season, black swans prefer shallow ponds, lakes, and swamps. The rest of the year, they are more often found in saltwater lakes and coastal habitats. Black swans are mainly herbivores, eating algae and different kinds of aquatic plants and weeds.

FAMILY & SOCIAL LIFE
Black swans can mate for life and usually live in pairs. They can also form large groups, especially during molting season, when they shed old feathers and grow new ones. During this time, they are without feathers and can't fly.

FUN FACT
During breeding season, a black swan's eyes, which are normally white, turn red.

BROLGA

ALL ABOUT

Brolgas are gray with a red band around their head. They are best known for the elaborate dances they perform during breeding season.

- **Height:** 3 to 4 feet (0.9 to 1.2 m)
- **Weight:** 10.6 to 19.2 pounds (4.8 to 8.7 kg)
- **Lifespan:** about 30 years
- **Conservation Status:** Least Concern

> **FUN FACT**
> Brolgas are thought to mate for life.

HABITAT & DIET

Brolgas are found across northern and eastern Australia, most commonly living in open wetlands, grassy plains, and coastal mudflats. Brolgas are omnivores that eat a variety of plants, insects, and amphibians.

FAMILY & SOCIAL LIFE

Brolgas often gather in large family groups of up to 100 birds. Unlike many birds, brolgas don't migrate. They've been known to use the same nesting area for up to 20 years.

BUDGERIGAR

ALL ABOUT

Budgerigars, nicknamed budgies, are small green-and-yellow parrots. They often have blue tail feathers and black markings across their head and wings.

- **Height:** 7 to 8 inches (17.8 to 20.3 cm)
- **Weight:** 1.1 to 1.4 ounces (30 to 40 g)
- **Lifespan:** 5 to 8 years
- **Conservation Status:** Least Concern

HABITAT & DIET

Budgerigars live mostly in semiarid regions of central Australia, but they can also be found in dry grasslands. They're herbivores that eat mainly seeds and grasses.

FUN FACT

Budgerigars can mimic human speech.

FAMILY & SOCIAL LIFE

Budgerigars sometimes live in flocks of up to tens of thousands of birds. Usually, though, they're found in smaller flocks that can range in size from just a few to 100.

CASSOWARY

ALL ABOUT

Cassowaries are large, flightless birds with long, powerful legs. Their talons are nearly 5 inches (12.7 cm) long. Cassowaries can deliver strong, deadly kicks when threatened.

   Cassowaries have a distinct, blade-like casque, sometimes called a helmet, on their head. The casque is made of a spongelike material and covered with keratin.

- **Height:** 4 to 5.5 feet (1.2 to 1.7 m)
- **Lifespan:** 50 to 60 years (under human care)
- **Weight:** up to 167 pounds (75.7 kg)
- **Conservation Status:** Least Concern

HABITAT & DIET

Cassowaries live in tropical forests and wetlands across northern Australia. They sometimes eat insects and snails, but they are mainly frugivores, eating fruit that has fallen off of trees.

   Cassowaries' poop often contains fruit seeds that are only partially digested. This helps scatter seeds throughout their ecosystem. There are certain plant seeds that are more likely to sprout after first passing through the cassowary's digestive system.

> **DID YOU KNOW?**
> The cassowary's distinct call is so low, wildlife specialists have reported feeling the rumble of it in their bones.

FAMILY & SOCIAL LIFE

Female cassowaries lay eggs, but it's the males who sit on the nest to incubate them. Once the babies hatch, they stay with their father for about 9 to 10 months.

FUN FACT

Cassowaries can run up to 31 miles per hour (49.9 kmh).

EMU

ALL ABOUT
Emus are the largest bird found in Australia. These flightless birds have dark to light gray feathers and bright red eyes. Their long, powerful legs help them run up to 30 miles per hour (48.3 kmh).
- **Height:** 5 to 6 feet (1.5 to 1.8 m)
- **Weight:** up to 120 pounds (54.4 kg)
- **Lifespan:** 10 to 20 years
- **Conservation Status:** Least Concern

HABITAT & DIET
Emus are found all over Australia, mainly living in sclerophyll forests or savanna woodlands. They are omnivores that eat fruit, seeds, and plants, as well as insects and other small animals.

FAMILY & SOCIAL LIFE
Like cassowaries, male emus are responsible for incubating and protecting unhatched eggs.

FUN FACT
Emus swallow large pebbles that help grind food in their stomach.

GALAH

ALL ABOUT
Galahs are also known as rose-breasted cockatoos. They have gray wings with a head and body that are various shades of pink.
- **Height:** 14 to 15 inches (35.6 to 38.1 cm)
- **Weight:** 10 to 12.2 ounces (283.5 to 345.9 g)
- **Lifespan:** about 25 years
- **Conservation Status:** Least Concern

HABITAT & DIET
Galahs are one of the most abundant bird species in Australia. They usually live in habitats with plenty of trees and water. Galahs eat seeds, nuts, berries, and grubs.

FAMILY & SOCIAL LIFE
Galahs are often spotted in large flocks of up to 1,000 birds. They mate for life. Both parents take care of the chicks.

FUN FACT
Male galahs have brown eyes, whereas females have red eyes.

GOULDIAN FINCH

ALL ABOUT
Gouldian finches are sometimes called rainbow finches due to their bright coloring. These small birds have a red, black, or yellow head with a turquoise band. Their wings and back are green, purple, and blue, and their belly is bright yellow.

- **Height:** 5.5 to 6 inches (14 to 15.2 cm)
- **Weight:** about 0.5 ounces (14.2 g)
- **Lifespan:** about 5 years
- **Conservation Status:** Least Concern

HABITAT & DIET
Gouldian finches are found around the coast of Australia, preferring open plains and tall eucalyptus trees. For most of the year, their diet is almost entirely grass seeds. During breeding season, however, they eat mostly insects.

FAMILY & SOCIAL LIFE
Gouldian finches usually make their nests in tree hollows. Several pairs often share one hollow.

FUN FACT
Only male Gouldian finches sing.

LAUGHING KOOKABURRA

ALL ABOUT
Laughing kookaburras are brown-and-gray birds with light blue patches on their wing feathers. Their unique call begins and ends with a low chuckle, with a sound like shrieking laughter in the middle.
- **Height:** 15 to 16.5 inches (38.1 to 41.9 cm)
- **Weight:** 6.7 to 16.4 ounces (190 to 464.9 g)
- **Lifespan:** 11 to 15 years
- **Conservation Status:** Least Concern

HABITAT & DIET
Laughing kookaburras can be found in the woodlands of eastern and southwestern Australia. They dine on a variety of insects, reptiles, frogs, and rodents.

DID YOU KNOW?
Laughing kookaburras can kill a snake up to 3 feet (0.9 m) long.

FAMILY & SOCIAL LIFE
Laughing kookaburras mate for life. When the chicks grow up, they stay near their parents. They help care for younger siblings during the next breeding season.

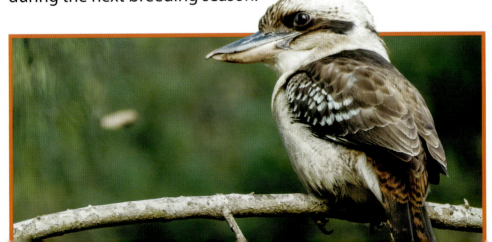

LITTLE PENGUIN

ALL ABOUT

Little penguins are the world's smallest species of penguins. They're also the only penguins with blue feathers. Dark feathers on their back and light feathers on their stomach help them camouflage, keeping them safe from predators swimming above or below.

> **FUN FACT**
> Little penguins only sleep for about four minutes at a time.

- **Height:** 13 to 15 inches (33 to 38.1 cm)
- **Weight:** 2 to 3 pounds (0.9 to 1.4 kg)
- **Lifespan:** about 6 years
- **Conservation Status:** Least Concern

HABITAT & DIET

Little penguins are found all along the southern coast of Australia and nearby islands. They prefer areas with rocks and sand.

Despite their size, little penguins are good hunters. They eat a variety of fish, squid, and krill. Little penguins leave land to hunt in the ocean at dawn and return at dusk.

FAMILY & SOCIAL LIFE

Little penguins form lifelong partnerships. Male penguins attract females by building a nest or rebuilding the nest from the previous year. Males usually build nests in underground burrows or in the cracks between rocks. Both the male and female take turns incubating the eggs.

DID YOU KNOW?

To ward off predators, little penguins shoot their poop up to 20 inches (50.8 cm), allowing them to stay safe while also keeping their home clean.

PEREGRINE FALCON

ALL ABOUT

Peregrine falcons are large birds of prey. They have dark gray to black feathers on their back and white or tan feathers with black markings on their chest.

- **Height:** 14 to 19 inches (35.6 to 48.3 cm)
- **Weight:** 1.25 to 2.75 pounds (0.6 to 1.2 kg)
- **Lifespan:** up to 17 years
- **Conservation Status:** Least Concern

DID YOU KNOW?

Peregrine falcons are the world's fastest diving bird. They've been recorded diving up to 186 miles (299.3 km) per hour.

HABITAT & DIET

Peregrine falcons are found across Australia. They live in a wide range of habitats, from rainforests to mountains. As carnivores, they mainly eat smaller birds but will sometimes eat fish, bats, or rodents.

FAMILY & SOCIAL LIFE

Both male and female peregrine falcons help take care of their young. The female incubates the eggs while the male hunts for food. Once the eggs hatch, both parents hunt and feed the chicks.

REGENT BOWERBIRD

ALL ABOUT
Male regent bowerbirds have a jet-black body with a bright yellow head and wingtips. Females are brown with black-and-white spots on their stomach.

- **Height:** 10 to 12 inches (25.4 to 30.5 cm)
- **Weight:** 2.7 to 4.9 ounces (76 to 139 g)
- **Lifespan:** 20 to 30 years
- **Conservation Status:** Least Concern

HABITAT & DIET
Regent bowerbirds are found in the forests on the eastern coast of Australia. They are frugivores, mostly eating fruit. They sometimes eat insects too.

> **DID YOU KNOW?**
>
> Each species of bowerbird prefers to decorate their bowers in a specific color. Regent bowerbirds use reddish-black or yellowish-brown objects.

FAMILY & SOCIAL LIFE
To attract a female partner, male regent bowerbirds build bowers, domed tunnels made of sticks. Bowers are decorated with small, colorful objects, such as flowers, stones, berries, and snail shells.

SPLENDID FAIRY-WREN

ALL ABOUT
Male splendid fairy-wrens are almost entirely bright blue in color, whereas females are gray and blue.
- **Height:** 4.7 to 5.5 inches (11.9 to 14 cm)
- **Weight:** 0.3 to 0.4 ounces (8.5 to 11.3 g)
- **Lifespan:** 5 to 6 years
- **Conservation Status:** Least Concern

HABITAT & DIET
Splendid fairy-wrens are found throughout Australia. They live in arid or semiarid areas with dense shrublands or woodlands. The splendid fairy-wren's diet is mostly insects.

FUN FACT
Males present females with pink or purple flower petals during mating season.

FAMILY & SOCIAL LIFE
Splendid fairy-wren mothers incubate the eggs after they're laid. Fathers help feed the chicks after they've hatched. As they get older, chicks often stay with their parents to help feed younger siblings.

TAWNY FROGMOUTH

ALL ABOUT
Tawny frogmouths are nocturnal birds that are often confused for owls. They have fluffy brown, gray, and black feathers. Their name comes from their wide beak that looks similar to a frog's mouth.

- **Height:** 8 to 21 inches (20.3 to 53.3 cm)
- **Weight:** 6.3 to 24 ounces (178 to 680.4 g)
- **Lifespan:** up to 14 years
- **Conservation Status:** Least Concern

FUN FACT
Tawny frogmouths have a long tongue that is forked at the end.

HABITAT & DIET
Tawny frogmouths are found throughout Australia. They can live in almost any habitat and are often seen in heath, forests, and woodlands. Tawny frogmouths mainly eat insects, worms, slugs, and snails.

FAMILY & SOCIAL LIFE
Like many birds, tawny frogmouths form bonds for life. Males and females both help incubate and care for the eggs.

WEDGE-TAILED EAGLE

ALL ABOUT
Wedge-tailed eagles are Australia's largest bird of prey. They have a wingspan up to 6 feet (1.8 m).
- **Height:** 2.6 to 3.3 feet (0.8 to 1 m)
- **Weight:** up to 11.7 pounds (5.3 kg)
- **Lifespan:** about 40 years
- **Conservation Status:** Least Concern

FUN FACT
The nests of wedge-tailed eagles can be nearly 6 feet (1.8 m) across.

HABITAT & DIET
Wedge-tailed eagles are abundant across all of Australia. They usually live in woodlands or forests, where they build their nests in the tallest trees. Wedge-tailed eagles mostly eat carrion. They'll also eat rabbits, lizards, and small birds and mammals.

FAMILY & SOCIAL LIFE
Wedge-tailed eagles mate for life. Pairs share the responsibilities of building nests, incubating the eggs, and feeding the young.

YELLOW-TAILED BLACK COCKATOO

ALL ABOUT
As their name suggests, yellow-tailed black cockatoos are mostly black with yellow spots on their tail and cheeks.
- **Height:** 22 to 25.5 inches (55.9 to 64.8 cm)
- **Weight:** 1.7 to 2 pounds (0.8 to 0.9 kg)
- **Lifespan:** 40 to 60 years
- **Conservation Status:** Least Concern

HABITAT & DIET
Yellow-tailed black cockatoos are found along the southeastern and central eastern coast of Australia. They can live in a wide range of habitats but prefer eucalyptus forests. They eat insect larvae and seeds.

FAMILY & SOCIAL LIFE
Male and female yellow-tailed black cockatoos build their nests together. The female incubates the eggs while the male brings her food.

FUN FACT
These birds peel back tree bark to get to the insects underneath.

BIRDS
ADDITIONAL BIRDS

AUSTRALIAN MAGPIE
- **About:** This bird can mimic the calls of more than 35 other bird species.
- **Habitat:** forests, savannas, grasslands
- **Conservation Status:** Least Concern

BLACK-BREASTED BUZZARD
- **About:** This bird uses a rock to crack open an egg to eat.
- **Habitat:** forests, savannas, shrublands, grasslands, deserts
- **Conservation Status:** Least Concern

Australian magpie

BLACK-NECKED STORK
- **About:** The black-necked stork is the only stork in Australia.
- **Habitat:** grasslands, wetlands, forests
- **Conservation Status:** Near Threatened

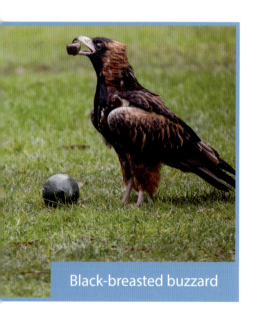
Black-breasted buzzard

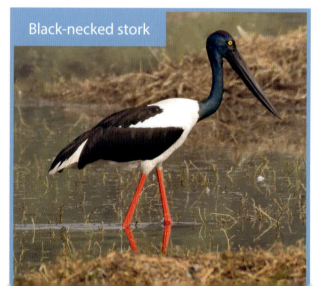
Black-necked stork

GOLDEN-HEADED CISTICOLA

- **About:** This bird builds spherical nests with an opening near the top.
- **Habitat:** savannas, shrublands, grasslands
- **Conservation Status:** Least Concern

Golden-headed cisticola

SUPERB LYREBIRD

- **About:** Eighty percent of this bird's song consists of sounds it hears and mimics.
- **Habitat:** forests
- **Conservation Status:** Least Concern

TASMANIAN NATIVE HEN

- **About:** This bird is only found on the island of Tasmania.
- **Habitat:** grasslands, wetlands
- **Conservation Status:** Least Concern

Superb lyrebird

Tasmanian native hen

FISH AND OTHER MARINE LIFE

An estimated 50 to 80 percent of all Earth's animals are found in the ocean. But only 10 percent of the ocean has been explored by humans. Scientists think there could be as many as 2.2 million marine species, but only about 240,000 have been discovered.

Most marine species are invertebrates. This includes mollusks, crustaceans, and Cnidaria. Mollusks are animals with soft bodies, sometimes protected by hard shells. Mollusks include gastropods (such as snails and slugs), cephalopods (such as octopuses and cuttlefish), and bivalves (such as clams and oysters).

Crustaceans are animals with hard exoskeletons. Their skeletons are on the outside of their bodies. These include crabs, lobsters, krill, and shrimp.

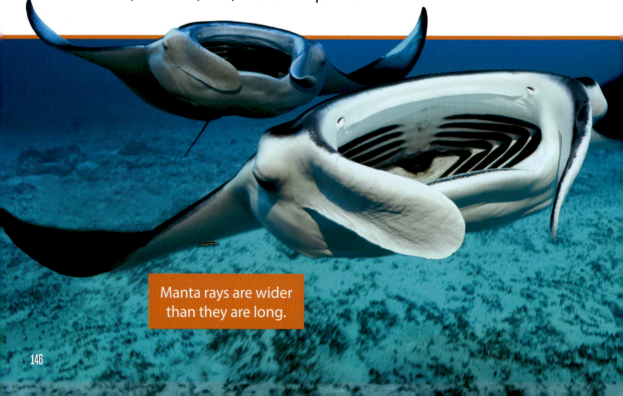

Manta rays are wider than they are long.

Cnidarians are soft-bodied animals with stinging tentacles. They have two basic forms: medusa and polyp. Medusae, such as jellyfish, float in the water, whereas polyps, such as sea anemone, are immobile.

Fish, including sharks and rays, are vertebrates. Fish species can vary widely in size, appearance, diet, reproduction, and habitats. There are about 34,000 species of fish in the world today.

Weedy seadragons are one of three species of seadragons in Australia.

AUSTRALIAN GIANT CUTTLEFISH

ALL ABOUT

The Australian giant cuttlefish is the largest of the more than 120 species of cuttlefish. Cuttlefish have eight arms and two long tentacles on their head. Like other cephalopods, giant cuttlefish can change the color, texture, and pattern of their skin.

- **Length:** up to 3 feet (0.9 m)
- **Weight:** up to 24.3 pounds (11 kg)
- **Lifespan:** 1 to 2 years
- **Conservation Status:** Near Threatened

FUN FACT
Giant cuttlefish have three hearts.

HABITAT & DIET

Giant cuttlefish are found in tropical and temperate waters around the southern coast of Australia. They live in reefs, kelp forests, and seagrass meadows. Giant cuttlefish generally stay in shallow water where the sun can reach them. However, they do sometimes venture up to 2,000 feet (609.6 m) underwater.

As carnivores, giant cuttlefish catch their prey with their tentacles and use their beak to crack open hard shells. Their diet consists of small fish and crustaceans, such as crabs and prawns.

DID YOU KNOW?
The cuttlefish's skin contains about 10 million color cells. The giant cuttlefish can control these cells to change the appearance of its skin.

FAMILY & SOCIAL LIFE

Cuttlefish mostly live alone, except during mating season. The male attracts a female by changing its color or pattern. Soon after cuttlefish reproduce, they die.

BARRIER REEF ANEMONEFISH

ALL ABOUT

Also known as clownfish, the Barrier Reef anemonefish is brownish orange with two vertical stripes and a white hind fin.

- **Length:** 2 to 5 inches (5.1 to 12.7 cm)
- **Weight:** about 1 ounce (28.3 g)
- **Lifespan:** 6 to 10 years
- **Conservation Status:** Least Concern

DID YOU KNOW?

Anemone tentacles are poisonous, but Barrier Reef anemonefish aren't affected.

HABITAT & DIET

These fish are found in the Great Barrier Reef along the northeast coast of Australia. They make their home among the tentacles of anemones. Barrier Reef anemonefish eat algae and a variety of small invertebrates.

FAMILY & SOCIAL LIFE

Anemonefish live in groups of several male fish and one dominant female. Females can lay thousands of eggs. Once the eggs are laid, males are mostly responsible for taking care of them.

BLUESPOTTED FANTAIL RAY

ALL ABOUT
Bluespotted fantail rays have an oval disc and a long tail. They're easily recognized by the bright blue spots on their disc and fins. They also have a stripe along either side of their tail.
- **Length:** up to 28 inches (71.1 cm)
- **Weight:** up to 11 pounds (5 kg)
- **Lifespan:** unknown
- **Conservation Status:** Least Concern

HABITAT & DIET
Bluespotted fantail rays are found in the shallow tropical waters around the northern coast of Australia. They're carnivores and dine on a variety of mollusks, worms, crustaceans, and small fish.

FAMILY & SOCIAL LIFE
Bluespotted fantail rays are known to travel in large schools into shallow waters to feed.

FUN FACT
Bluespotted fantail rays can be found as far as 66 feet (20.1 m) underwater.

COMMON SYDNEY OCTOPUS

ALL ABOUT

The common Sydney octopus is usually gray and brown with reddish-brown arms. However, it has the ability to change its skin color and texture in a matter of seconds. This helps it imitate seaweed and blend into its environment.

- **Arm Span:** up to 6.6 feet (2 m)
- **Weight:** up to 5.7 pounds (2.6 kg)
- **Lifespan:** 2 to 3 years
- **Conservation Status:** Least Concern

DID YOU KNOW?

The common Sydney octopus is territorial. It builds a lair among rocks and will collect debris to help defend its home.

HABITAT & DIET

Common Sydney octopuses are found along the eastern and southern coasts of Australia. They are carnivores and eat crabs, lobsters, and fish. They grab their prey with their arms and use their sharp, beak-like mouth to crush their prey's shell.

FAMILY & SOCIAL LIFE

The common Sydney octopus mostly lives alone, except in the breeding season. During this time, female octopuses lay up to 100,000 eggs, guarding them until they hatch. After mating, a female octopus might eat the male.

FUN FACT

Common Sydney octopuses have bluish-green blood.

GIANT CLAM

ALL ABOUT

The giant clam is the largest bivalve mollusk in the world. It can be many different colors, depending on the algae inside it and its natural pigment.

> **FUN FACT**
> The largest giant clam ever found weighed 550 pounds (249.5 kg).

- **Length:** up to 4 feet (1.2 m)
- **Weight:** can be more than 440 pounds (200 kg)
- **Lifespan:** 100 years or more
- **Conservation Status:** Vulnerable

HABITAT & DIET

Giant clams are found in the Great Barrier Reef. They live about 66 feet (20.1 m) below water and remain attached to the reef their entire life.

Giant clams eat the sugars and proteins produced by the algae that live in their tissue. In return, the clams open during the day, giving the algae inside access to sunlight for photosynthesis. Giant clams also filter feed, drawing in water and filtering it back out while trapping plankton inside.

FAMILY & SOCIAL LIFE

Giant clams produce both eggs and sperm. A fully grown clam can release more than 500 million eggs at once. However, clams can't fertilize their own eggs. Instead, an egg release triggers a nearby clam to open and take in the sperm and eggs to fertilize them.

DID YOU KNOW?

A giant clam's colors can be a sign of its health. Vibrant colors indicate good health. If the clam is dull and white, it's unhealthy.

GREAT WHITE SHARK

ALL ABOUT
Great white sharks are the world's largest predatory fish. They have a torpedo-shaped body that allows them to swim up to 35 miles per hour (56.3 kmh). Despite their name, these sharks are only white on the bottom. On top, they're usually light brown or gray. This coloring helps them blend into their environment.
- **Length:** up to 21 feet (6.4 m)
- **Weight:** up to 1,500 to 4,000 pounds (680.4 to 1,814.4 kg)
- **Lifespan:** 70 or more years
- **Conservation Status:** Vulnerable

HABITAT & DIET
Great white sharks are found in temperate and tropical waters around the world, including all along the Australian coast. Their carnivorous diet changes as they age. Young sharks eat smaller prey, such as crustaceans, mollusks, and sea birds. Older sharks eat sea lions, seals, dolphins, and even smaller great white sharks.

DID YOU KNOW?
Great white sharks continue to grow new teeth throughout their life.

FAMILY & SOCIAL LIFE
Female great white sharks give birth to live pups once every two to three years. At birth, pups can be up to 6 feet (1.8 m) long.

FUN FACT
A fully grown great white shark can weigh more than 4,500 pounds (2,041.2 kg).

HAMMERHEAD SHARK

ALL ABOUT
Hammerhead sharks are known for their uniquely shaped head. They use their wide-set eyes to scan their surroundings for food. Special sensory organs on their head help the sharks detect electrical fields created by prey.
- **Length:** 13 to 20 feet (4 to 6.1 m)
- **Weight:** up to 1,102.3 pounds (500 kg)
- **Lifespan:** 20 to 30 years
- **Conservation Status:** Critically Endangered

FUN FACT
A hammerhead shark's preferred prey is stingrays.

HABITAT & DIET
Hammerhead sharks can be found in the temperate and tropical waters off the northern coast of Australia. These carnivores dine on a variety of fish, crustaceans, and cephalopods.

FAMILY & SOCIAL LIFE
Hammerhead sharks live alone, except during breeding season. Female hammerheads give birth to live pups.

FISH AND OTHER MARINE LIFE

HOODWINKER SUNFISH

ALL ABOUT

The large hoodwinker sunfish doesn't have a caudal fin—the very back fin of a fish. Instead, it has a rudder-like structure that helps it steer through the water.

- **Length:** up to 9 feet (2.7 m)
- **Weight:** up to 4,400 pounds (1,995.8 kg)
- **Lifespan:** unknown
- **Conservation Status:** Not Assessed

FUN FACT
Hoodwinker sunfish grow more than 60 million times their birth size.

HABITAT & DIET

Hoodwinker sunfish are found along the southern coast of Australia. They're omnivores that eat plants and animals such as jellyfish. They can dive more than 1,968 feet (599.8 m) to find food.

FAMILY & SOCIAL LIFE

Female hoodwinker sunfish produce about 300 million eggs in a single breeding season. Young fish swim in groups for protection. Adult hoodwinker sunfish live alone.

LEAFY SEADRAGON

ALL ABOUT

Leafy seadragons are one of the best-camouflaged species in the world. These creatures are covered in leaflike structures as well as hard, bony plates with sharp spikes, which can be used to defend against predators.

> **DID YOU KNOW?**
> Leafy seadragons don't have teeth. They eat by sucking in their prey and swallowing it whole.

The color of leafy seadragons can vary. Those living in shallow water are usually yellowish brown, whereas those in deep water are dark brown or red.

- **Length:** up to 14 inches (35.6 cm)
- **Weight:** about 0.3 pounds (0.1 kg)
- **Lifespan:** about 7 to 10 years
- **Conservation Status:** Least Concern

HABITAT & DIET

Leafy seadragons can be found around the southern and western coasts of Australia. They live in rock reefs close to kelp or seaweed beds. Leafy seadragons eat small shrimp and other crustaceans, plankton, and baby fish.

FAMILY & SOCIAL LIFE

During breeding season, the female seadragon lays between 250 and 300 eggs, but it's the male who incubates them. The female pushes the eggs into the soft skin of the male. The male's skin hardens around the eggs to keep them safe for up to eight weeks. When they start to hatch, he releases them.

FUN FACT

Leafy seadragons are named after the dragons in Chinese mythology.

FISH AND OTHER MARINE LIFE

MANTA RAY

ALL ABOUT

The largest rays in the world, manta rays have large, flat, diamond-shaped bodies and two horn-shaped fins. There are two species of manta rays: the reef manta ray and the giant manta ray.

Manta rays are smart and may have excellent long-term memories. They can create mental maps of their environment.

- **Length:** up to 26 feet (7.9 m)
- **Weight:** up to 5,300 pounds (2,404 kg)
- **Lifespan:** up to 45 years
- **Conservation Status:** Endangered

> **FUN FACT**
> *Manta* means "blanket" or "cloak" in Spanish.

HABITAT & DIET

Manta rays live in tropical, subtropical, and temperate ocean waters. They can be found along the northern coast of Australia. Manta rays are filter feeders, dining on plankton and krill. Manta rays sometimes follow each other in a circle with their mouth open. This creates a mini cyclone, trapping prey.

FAMILY & SOCIAL LIFE

Manta rays live alone but sometimes gather in small groups to feed. They also regularly visit cleaning stations on coral reefs. There, larger animals stay still for several minutes while small fish remove parasites and dead skin.

> **DID YOU KNOW?**
> The markings on the underside of a manta ray are unique to each one, similar to a fingerprint.

MĀORI WRASSE

ALL ABOUT

The Māori wrasse is also known as the humphead wrasse because of the large lump on its forehead. Māori wrasses can be many different colors, from electric blue to red and orange.

- **Length:** up to 6 feet (1.8 m)
- **Weight:** up to 286.6 pounds (130 kg)
- **Lifespan:** more than 30 years
- **Conservation Status:** Endangered

FUN FACT

Māori wrasses are one of the largest reef fish in the world.

HABITAT & DIET

Māori wrasses are found around the northern coast of Australia, usually living among reefs. They eat a variety of mollusks, sea urchins, crustaceans, and fish.

FAMILY & SOCIAL LIFE

Māori wrasses normally live alone or in small groups. During breeding season, Māori wrasses gather in groups of up to 100 individuals.

SPOTTED HANDFISH

ALL ABOUT
The spotted handfish has fins that look like hands. Instead of swimming, they use their fins to "walk" across the ocean floor.
- **Length:** about 5 inches (12.7 cm)
- **Weight:** up to 0.4 ounces (11.3 g)
- **Lifespan:** unknown
- **Conservation Status:** Critically Endangered

HABITAT & DIET
The spotted handfish is only found in one location along the Great Southern Reef on the southeastern coast of Australia. Spotted handfish eat a variety of crustaceans, worms, and small shellfish.

FAMILY & SOCIAL LIFE
During breeding season, the female spotted handfish lays eggs on vertical objects such as sea sponges or grasses. She guards the eggs until they hatch.

FUN FACT
The pattern of spots on a spotted handfish are unique to each fish.

TIGER SHARK

ALL ABOUT

Tiger sharks are named for the distinct vertical stripes on the sides of their body. Like tigers, these sharks are fierce predators.

- **Length:** 10 to 18 feet (3 to 5.5 m)
- **Weight:** 700 to 2,000 pounds (317.5 to 907.2 kg)
- **Lifespan:** more than 30 years
- **Conservation Status:** Near Threatened

FUN FACT
Tiger sharks will hunt and eat prey for fun even when they aren't hungry.

HABITAT & DIET

Tiger sharks are mainly found in tropical and subtropical waters. They live off the eastern, northern, and western coasts of Australia. Tiger sharks eat a wide variety of food, including fish, sea turtles, stingrays, and sea mammals.

FAMILY & SOCIAL LIFE

Female tiger sharks give birth to live pups. Each embryo develops in its own egg and hatches inside the mother's body.

WEEDY SEADRAGON

ALL ABOUT
Weedy seadragons have a long, tubelike snout and a few small, weed-like structures coming off their body. They are usually red in color with yellow spots and blue stripes.
- **Length:** up to 18 inches (45.7 cm)
- **Weight:** not enough data
- **Lifespan:** about 5 to 7 years
- **Conservation Status:** Least Concern

> **FUN FACT**
> Despite being marine animals, weedy seadragons are poor swimmers.

HABITAT & DIET
Weedy seadragons can be found around the southern coast of Australia. They live in kelp along rocky reefs. Weedy seadragons eat a variety of small crustaceans.

FAMILY & SOCIAL LIFE
Weedy seadragons mostly live alone until breeding season. Like leafy seadragons, male weedy seadragons carry the eggs. Up to 250 babies can hatch at a time.

WHALE SHARK

ALL ABOUT

Whale sharks are gray or brown with white spots and stripes that are unique to each shark. Their mouth is about 4 feet (1.2 m) wide. They have more than 3,000 teeth.
- **Length:** 18 to 33 feet (5.5 to 10.1 m)
- **Weight:** up to 74,957 pounds (34,000 kg)
- **Lifespan:** 70 to 100 years
- **Conservation Status:** Endangered

HABITAT & DIET

These large sharks live in the warm, tropical waters around the northern coast of Australia. They tend to stay near the water's surface but can be found more than 3,280 feet (999.7 m) underwater.

Because of their size, whale sharks travel up to 5,000 miles (8,046.7 km) a year to find enough food to sustain them. They do not use their teeth to eat. Instead, they are filter feeders that eat mainly small sea creatures such as krill, crabs, fish, and jellyfish.

FUN FACT

Whale sharks have tiny teeth-like structures covering their eyeballs. These help protect their eyes from the harsh ocean environment.

FISH AND OTHER MARINE LIFE

FAMILY & SOCIAL LIFE

Whale sharks mostly live alone. However, they're sometimes seen hunting with other species of fish in the spring and summer.

Whale sharks are ovoviviparous. Their eggs hatch gradually over a period of time, rather than all at once.

DID YOU KNOW?

Despite being the largest sharks, whale sharks are known for being gentle creatures.

FISH AND OTHER MARINE LIFE
ADDITIONAL FISH AND OTHER MARINE LIFE

BLUE TANG
- **About:** This fish has a pair of razor-sharp, venomous spines on its tail.
- **Habitat:** coral reefs, estuaries
- **Conservation Status:** Least Concern

Blue tang

Greater blue-ringed octopus

Horned blenny

GREATER BLUE-RINGED OCTOPUS
- **About:** This octopus's venom is extremely toxic.
- **Habitat:** marine waters
- **Conservation Status:** Least Concern

HORNED BLENNY
- **About:** This fish has two hornlike tentacles above its eyes.
- **Habitat:** coral reefs
- **Conservation Status:** Least Concern

Port Jackson shark

PORT JACKSON SHARK
- **About:** Unlike most sharks, this shark can eat and breathe at the same time.
- **Habitat:** marine waters
- **Conservation Status:** Least Concern

PORTUGUESE MAN-OF-WAR
- **About:** This creature's tentacles can be up to 165 feet (50.3 m) long.
- **Habitat:** warm oceans
- **Conservation Status:** Not Assessed

Portuguese man-of-war

TASSELLED WOBBEGONG
- **About:** This shark's coloring helps it blend into its surroundings.
- **Habitat:** marine waters
- **Conservation Status:** Least Concern

Tasselled wobbegong

INSECTS AND SPIDERS

Insects are arthropods with six jointed legs, a body with three segments, an exoskeleton, a pair of antennae, and zero to two pairs of wings. Insects are found in nearly every habitat in the world. Scientists have named one million insect species so far, but there are millions more that haven't been named.

Spiders are a type of arthropod called arachnids. They have eight jointed legs and a body made up of two segments. They don't have antennae or wings like insects do. There are more than 46,700 known species of spiders in the world.

Insects and spiders reproduce by either laying eggs or carrying eggs that hatch inside the female's body. When spiders hatch, they are smaller versions of adult spiders. Insects, however, go through a metamorphosis, which is a physical change with three or four distinct stages.

Christmas beetles have spiky legs and clubbed antennae that help them grip leaves as they eat.

Atlas moths are large, up to 10 inches (25.4 cm) wide.

AUSTRALIAN TARANTULA

ALL ABOUT
All species of Australian tarantulas have large, heavy bodies that vary in color from dark brown to light brown, with a silvery sheen. Australian tarantulas also have fangs.
- **Leg Span:** up to 6 inches (15.2 cm)
- **Weight:** 1 to 3 ounces (28.3 to 85 g)
- **Lifespan:** up to 12 years
- **Conservation Status:** Not Assessed

HABITAT & DIET
Australian tarantulas live in a range of habitats, from rainforests to deserts throughout northeastern Australia. Female tarantulas live in web-lined underground burrows that can be anywhere from 15 to 40 inches (38.1 to 101.6 cm) deep. Males most commonly live under rocks or logs.

Australian tarantulas are carnivores that eat insects, lizards, and other spiders. They occasionally snatch baby birds from nests on the ground to eat too.

FAMILY & SOCIAL LIFE
During breeding season, males must draw females out of their burrows to mate. The female will lay about 50 eggs in her burrow, protected by a tough layer of silk.

FUN FACT
Instead of chewing, these spiders liquify their prey using venom.

DID YOU KNOW?

Australian tarantulas are also called whistling or barking tarantulas because of the distinct sounds they make to scare off predators.

CABBAGE WHITE BUTTERFLY

ALL ABOUT

Cabbage white butterflies have white wings with black tips. Females have two black dots in the middle of their wings, whereas males have just one.

- **Wingspan:** 1.8 to 2.6 inches (4.6 to 6.6 cm)
- **Weight:** not enough data
- **Lifespan:** 3 to 6 weeks
- **Conservation Status:** Not Assessed

HABITAT & DIET

Cabbage white butterflies are found throughout Australia, but especially in the southeast. They can live in a wide range of habitats such as forests, fields, and meadows. They dine on plant nectar.

FAMILY & SOCIAL LIFE

Females lay their eggs on the undersides of plant leaves. One plant can have up to 57 eggs and 48 larvae on it at a time.

DID YOU KNOW?

As larvae, the preferred food of cabbage white butterflies is the leafy cabbage plant.

CAIRNS BIRDWING BUTTERFLY

ALL ABOUT

The Cairns birdwing butterfly is the largest butterfly in Australia. The male of the species is very colorful, with blue, green, and gold on its wings and red on its body. Females are black and white with some yellow.

- **Wingspan:** up to 10 inches (25.4 cm)
- **Weight:** not enough data
- **Lifespan:** 4 to 5 weeks
- **Conservation Status:** Least Concern

FUN FACT
Female Cairns birdwing butterflies are bigger than the males.

HABITAT & DIET

Cairns birdwing butterflies are found in the rainforests of northeastern Australia. They feed on tropical vines and plants found in their habitat.

FAMILY & SOCIAL LIFE

Female butterflies lay their eggs on a host plant, which provides food for the caterpillars as they grow.

CHRISTMAS BEETLE

ALL ABOUT

There are 36 species of Christmas beetles, all but one of which are found only in Australia. Christmas beetles are shiny and can be vibrantly colored.

- **Length:** 1 to 1.2 inches (2.5 to 3 cm)
- **Weight:** not enough data
- **Lifespan:** 2 years
- **Conservation Status:** Not Assessed

DID YOU KNOW?

Many Christmas beetles emerge from their pupa stage in late December.

HABITAT & DIET

Christmas beetles are found in eastern and southern Australia. They live in forests and woodland areas where they feed mainly on eucalyptus leaves.

FAMILY & SOCIAL LIFE

Christmas beetles often gather by the hundreds in a single tree to eat and find mates. Female beetles lay their eggs underground where the larvae can feed on grass roots.

GIANT BURROWING COCKROACH

ALL ABOUT
Giant burrowing cockroaches are the heaviest, and one of the longest, cockroaches in the world. They have a reddish-brown exoskeleton. Males have a flat, shovel-shaped head, which they use for digging.
- **Length:** up to 3 inches (7.6 cm)
- **Weight:** up to 1.2 ounces (34 g)
- **Lifespan:** up to 10 years
- **Conservation Status:** Not Assessed

FUN FACT
Unlike most insects, the giant burrowing cockroach doesn't have wings.

HABITAT & DIET
Giant burrowing cockroaches are found in the forests of northeastern Australia, spending most of their time underground. They eat dry leaves, twigs, and bark.

FAMILY & SOCIAL LIFE
Female giant burrowing cockroaches give birth to live young. The young stay with their mother for many months before leaving her burrow to make their own.

GIANT PRICKLY STICK INSECT

ALL ABOUT
The giant prickly stick insect looks just like a prickly stick. However, its shape and color change to match its environment.
- **Length:** up to 8 inches (20.3 cm)
- **Weight:** not enough data
- **Lifespan:** 6 to 18 months
- **Conservation Status:** Least Concern

DID YOU KNOW?
Females are covered in thornlike spikes, which protect them from predators.

HABITAT & DIET
Giant prickly stick insects are found in northwestern Australia. They make their homes in eucalyptus trees where they dine on leaves.

FAMILY & SOCIAL LIFE
Giant prickly stick insect eggs look like seeds. Spider ants collect the eggs and take them to the ant colony where the outer layer is eaten. When the eggs hatch, the babies look like spider ants and leave the colony without being bothered.

GIANT WATER BUG

ALL ABOUT
When hunting, giant water bugs position themselves head down in the water and breathe using a tube on their rear end that acts as a snorkel.
- **Length:** up to 3 inches (7.6 cm)
- **Weight:** up to 2 ounces (56.7 g)
- **Lifespan:** 1 to 2 years
- **Conservation Status:** Not Assessed

FUN FACT
Giant water bugs capture their prey by grabbing it with their front legs.

HABITAT & DIET
Giant water bugs are found in eastern Australia. They live in still bodies of fresh water, such as lakes. Giant water bugs eat a variety of tadpoles, small fish, frogs, snails, and aquatic insects.

FAMILY & SOCIAL LIFE
Female giant water bugs lay up to 80 eggs on sticks or plant stems near water. Males protect the eggs until they hatch, which takes about 10 days.

GOLIATH STICK INSECT

ALL ABOUT

The goliath stick insect is one of the largest species of stick insects found in Australia. They are bright green with yellow patches.

- **Length:** up to 10 inches (25.4 cm)
- **Weight:** not enough data
- **Lifespan:** about 1 year
- **Conservation Status:** Least Concern

HABITAT & DIET

Goliath stick insects are found throughout northern and western Australia, making their homes primarily in woodlands and rainforests. They eat mostly acacia and eucalyptus leaves.

DID YOU KNOW?

Female goliath stick insects have wings, but they can't fly. However, if they fall out of a tree, their wings can act as a parachute.

FAMILY & SOCIAL LIFE

Eggs come out of a female's abdomen through a special chute. They then remain on the ground for about four to six months before hatching.

HERCULES MOTH

ALL ABOUT

The largest moth in the world, the Hercules moth has large wings of various shades of brown with white markings.

- **Wingspan:** up to 10.5 inches (26.7 cm)
- **Weight:** not enough data
- **Lifespan:** up to 3 months
- **Conservation Status:** Not Assessed

DID YOU KNOW?

The largest known Hercules moth had a wingspan of 14 inches (35.6 cm).

HABITAT & DIET

The Hercules moth is found in the tropical rainforests of northwestern Australia. These moths don't eat. Instead, they survive off the fat they built up as caterpillars.

FAMILY & SOCIAL LIFE

Hercules moths spend most of their lives as caterpillars. As full-grown moths, they only live for about two weeks, during which time they mate.

TRIANGULAR SPIDER

ALL ABOUT

Triangular spiders, named for their shape, are usually bright orange or red, with white, yellow, and black markings on their body.

- **Length:** 0.2 to 0.4 inches (0.5 to 1 cm)
- **Weight:** up to 0.02 ounces (0.5 g)
- **Lifespan:** unknown
- **Conservation Status:** Not Assessed

DID YOU KNOW?

Instead of catching prey in a web, triangular spiders ambush their prey, grabbing it with their front legs.

HABITAT & DIET

Triangular spiders are found throughout Australia, but are most common on the east coast. They usually live in eucalyptus forests and woodlands. Triangular spiders feed on small insects, especially flies.

FAMILY & SOCIAL LIFE

Female triangular spiders reproduce by laying an egg sac of about 50 eggs. They place the egg sac on the underside of plants low to the ground.

ULYSSES BUTTERFLY

ALL ABOUT
Because of its bright coloring, the Ulysses butterfly is easily detected. But this butterfly is able to ward off predators by flying quickly and frantically.

- **Wingspan:** 4 to 5 inches (10.2 to 12.7 cm)
- **Weight:** not enough data
- **Lifespan:** 2 to 4 weeks
- **Conservation Status:** Not Assessed

HABITAT & DIET
Ulysses butterflies are found in the tropical rainforests of northeastern Australia. They live below the rainforest canopy where they feed on the nectar of a variety of flowers.

FUN FACT
Ulysses butterflies are attracted to the color blue.

FAMILY & SOCIAL LIFE
Female Ulysses butterflies lay their eggs individually on the underside of plant leaves. After they hatch, the larvae eat the host plant until they're ready to pupate.

INSECTS AND SPIDERS
ADDITIONAL INSECTS AND SPIDERS

Australian emperor dragonfly

Australian golden orb weaver

AUSTRALIAN EMPEROR DRAGONFLY
- **About:** Females attach their eggs to plants in or near water.
- **Habitat:** shrublands, grasslands, wetlands
- **Conservation Status:** Least Concern

AUSTRALIAN GOLDEN ORB WEAVER
- **About:** These spiders build webs with a gold sheen.
- **Habitat:** forests, woodlands
- **Conservation Status:** Least Concern

BOGONG MOTH
- **About:** Each spring, these moths can travel up to 620 miles (997.8 km).
- **Habitat:** forests, savannas, shrublands, grasslands
- **Conservation Status:** Endangered

Bogong moth

MOUSE SPIDER

- **About:** These spiders live in burrows up to 22 inches (55.9 cm) deep.
- **Habitat:** forests, shrublands
- **Conservation Status:** Not Assessed

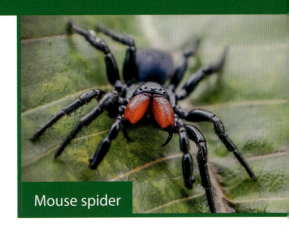
Mouse spider

Neon cuckoo bee

NEON CUCKOO BEE

- **About:** Instead of building their own nests, these bees lay their eggs in other bees' nests.
- **Habitat:** forests, woodlands, heath
- **Conservation Status:** Not Assessed

TRAP-DOOR SPIDER

- **About:** These spiders build webbed entrances to their burrows. The spiders quickly open their "doors" to catch prey walking by.
- **Habitat:** forests, wetlands
- **Conservation Status:** Varies by species

Trap-door spider

GLOSSARY

aquatic
Growing, living, or often found in water.

arid
Very dry; having little or no rain.

baleen
The bony, flexible strips in the upper jaws of whales that feed by filtering food from ocean water.

bivalve mollusk
A mollusk that has a shell made up of two parts joined by a hinge and lacking a distinct head.

carrion
Dead and decaying flesh.

crevice
A narrow, tight opening in a surface; a crack.

feral
Having escaped from domestication and become wild.

habitat
The type of place where a plant or animal naturally or normally lives.

heath
An area of flat land with low shrubs.

humid
Having a lot of moisture in the air.

invasive species
Species that are not native to a place, but grow and spread easily, usually causing harm to native species.

keratin
A protein that makes up hair, nails, horns, claws, quills, scales, and the outer layer of skin.

krill
Tiny, shrimplike fish.

mulga
A shrubby Australian acacia tree.

precipitation
Any liquid or frozen water that falls to the ground.

rostrum
A beak-like snout found on animals such as dolphins.

sclerophyll
Woody plants with evergreen leaves that have adapted to long periods of dryness and heat.

TO LEARN MORE

FURTHER READINGS

Chun, Matt. *Australian Animals*. Hardie Grant Children's Publishing, 2021.

Cronin, Leonard. *Wild Australian Life*. A&U Children, 2023.

Edward, Susan Bradford. *Australia*. Abdo Publishing, 2023.

London, Martha. *Great Barrier Reef*. Abdo Publishing, 2021.

Murray, Julie. *Kangaroos*. Abdo Publishing, 2020.

Reeder, Stephanie Owen. *Sensational Australian Animals*. CSIRO Publishing, 2024.

ONLINE RESOURCES

To learn more about Australian animals, please visit **abdobooklinks.com** or scan this QR code. These links are routinely monitored and updated to provide the most current information available.

INDEX

aggressive animals, 34, 65, 115
arid, 5, 77, 87, 90, 124, 140
Asia, 4, 15
Australian Outback, 5

baleen, 44, 48, 53
burrows, 19, 24, 38, 39, 73, 80, 84, 91, 95, 104, 136, 174, 179, 187

Cape York, 108
carnivores, 14, 18, 30, 45, 50, 51, 55, 57, 85, 87, 89, 94, 100, 105, 113, 114, 115, 125, 138, 148, 151, 152, 158, 174
carrion, 142
cephalopods, 146, 148, 158
coasts, 8, 30, 36, 41, 42, 44, 45, 46, 49, 50, 51, 52, 53, 54, 56, 69, 89, 96, 97, 98, 99, 100, 101, 104, 116, 117, 118, 124, 125, 126, 128, 134, 136, 139, 143, 148, 150, 151, 152, 156, 158, 159, 160, 163, 164, 165, 166, 167, 168, 184
communication, 14, 25, 33, 41, 44, 46, 49, 53, 55, 65, 69, 75, 76, 77, 92, 93, 122, 124, 125, 130, 135, 144, 145, 175

deserts, 5, 6, 16, 17, 31, 77, 80, 104, 112, 144, 174

eucalyptus, 12, 22, 25, 34, 58, 134, 143, 178, 180, 182, 184
extinction, 19

feral animals, 16
forests, 6, 13, 28, 30, 31, 33, 35, 36, 38, 58, 59, 69, 70, 76, 78, 79, 81, 82, 84, 102, 104, 106, 113, 117, 118, 119, 123, 130, 132, 139, 141, 142, 144, 145, 176, 178, 179, 186, 187
fresh water, 181

frugivores, 130, 139

grasslands, 6, 14, 17, 20, 25, 31, 38, 59, 66, 76, 80, 85, 106, 107, 111, 112, 113, 117, 118, 119, 122, 129, 144, 145, 186
Great Barrier Reef, 8, 9, 99, 100, 150, 154

hatchlings, 60, 73, 78, 82, 96, 105, 108, 109
heath, 6, 30, 36, 70, 76, 89, 106, 111, 141, 187
herbivores, 16, 20, 25, 28, 36, 37, 38, 46, 97, 126, 129

incubation, 82, 84, 103, 109, 120, 124, 131, 132, 136, 138, 140, 141, 142, 143, 160
invasive species, 16

Jardine River, 93

lagoons, 63, 64, 92, 113, 115

marshes, 67
marsupials, 18, 19, 20, 22, 25, 28, 32, 33, 34, 35, 37, 38, 58
migration, 49, 100, 128
molting, 126
mulga, 104, 112
mythology, 17, 161

omnivores, 31, 33, 75, 77, 78, 79, 80, 81, 88, 92, 93, 96, 98, 101, 122, 128, 132, 159
ovoviviparous animals, 111, 114, 169

poison, 68, 114, 118
poisonous animals, 22, 70, 150
predators, 14, 19, 24, 25, 28, 39, 68, 70, 79, 80, 82, 88, 90, 103, 104, 113, 119, 123, 136, 137, 156, 160, 166, 175, 180, 185

prey, 17, 26, 28, 50, 55, 63, 64, 65, 84, 87, 94, 100, 102, 103, 106, 107, 108, 138, 142, 148, 152, 156, 158, 160, 163, 166, 174, 181, 184, 187

rainforests, 6, 12, 25, 58, 75, 79, 102, 105, 108, 114, 123, 138, 174, 177, 182, 183, 185

salt water, 64, 65, 126
savannas, 6, 12, 20, 58, 59, 77, 82, 85, 102, 107, 118, 119, 125, 132, 144, 145, 186
sclerophyll, 123, 132
scrublands, 17, 20, 76, 77, 102, 103, 104, 107, 111, 112, 117
shrublands, 6, 18, 19, 28, 34, 37, 58, 59, 76, 80, 118, 119, 140, 144, 145, 186, 187
swamps, 36, 63, 64, 70, 94, 113, 115, 126

toxins, 22, 110, 170
tropical areas, 5, 35, 69, 75, 82, 92, 98, 102, 130, 148, 151, 156, 158, 163, 166, 168, 177, 183, 185

venom, 26, 27, 105, 108, 110, 114, 115, 170, 174
venomous animals, 26, 105, 107, 118, 170

wetlands, 6, 28, 58, 59, 94, 115, 118, 119, 128, 130, 144, 145, 186, 187
woodlands, 6, 12, 13, 14, 17, 18, 19, 30, 34, 70, 78, 81, 82, 88, 102, 104, 105, 106, 107, 111, 112, 113, 122, 125, 132, 135, 140, 141, 142, 178, 182, 184, 186, 187

PHOTO CREDITS

Cover photos: Sumruay Rattanataipob/Shutterstock, front (flying fox); alice-photo/Shutterstock, front (Ulysses butterfly); Songsak Pandet/Shutterstock, front (crocodile); GlobalP/iStock/Getty Images, front (emu); Anna Azimi/Shutterstock, front (blue tang); bradleyblackburn/iStock/Getty Images, front (kangaroo); Eric Isselee/Shutterstock, front (koala), front (bearded dragon), back (echidna); wallerichmercie/Shutterstock, front (Barrier Reef anemonefish); David Dennis/Shutterstock, front (little penguin); Dzikrul Husnani/Adobe Stock, front (great white shark); SeanScottPhotography/Shutterstock, back (green sea turtle); Matilda_Turner/Shutterstock, back (quokka)

Interior photos: Jami Tarris/Stone/Getty Images, 1; BenGoode/iStock/Getty Images, 4; Leelakajonkij/Moment/Getty Images, 5; Designua/Shutterstock, 6; Andrew Merry/Moment/Getty Images, 7 (top); Matteo Colombo/Moment/Getty Images, 7 (middle); John White Photos/Moment/Getty Images, 7 (bottom); Vlad61/Shutterstock, 8; Grant Faint/The Image Bank/Getty Images, 9; MB Photography/Moment/Getty Images, 10; Lea Scaddan/Moment/Getty Images, 11 (top), 24 (bottom), 120–121; Kristian Bell/Moment/Getty Images, 11 (bottom), 61 (top); DEA/C.DANI/I.JESKE/De Agostini/Getty Images, 12; Jason Roberts/500px/Getty Images, 13; Martin Harvey/The Image Bank/Getty Images, 15, 19; GISTEL Cezary Wojtkowski/iStock/Getty Images, 16, 128; Andrew Haysom/iStock/Getty Images, 17; Miropa/iStock/Getty Images, 18 (top), 18 (bottom), 58 (middle); Raimund Linke/The Image Bank/Getty Images, 20–21; Maridav/iStock/Getty Images, 22; Freder/iStock/Getty Images, 23; Jennifer A Smith/Moment/Getty Images, 24 (top); crbellette/Shutterstock, 25; phototrip/iStock/Getty Images, 26, 139, 140; slowmotiongli/iStock/Getty Images, 27; Westend61/Getty Images, 29; CraigRJD/iStock/Getty Images, 30 (top), 30 (bottom), 35 (bottom); 86, 86–87, 145 (middle); Greg Wyncoll/iStock/Getty Images, 31; Auscape International Pty Ltd/Alamy, 32; anisah_priyadi/RooM/Getty Images, 33; AustralianCamera/iStock/Getty Images, 34; kwiktor/iStock/Getty Images, 35 (top); Shmenny50/iStock/Getty Images, 36; Marion Springer/iStock/Getty Images, 37; 3sby/Shutterstock, 38; mlharing/iStock/Getty Images, 39; FiledIMAGE/Shutterstock, 40; Earth And More/Shutterstock, 41; Alastair Pollock Photography/Moment/Getty Images, 42, 157; richcarey/iStock/Getty Images, 43; Ajit S N/Shutterstock, 44; Martin Ruegner/Photographer's Choice RF/Getty Images, 45; cinoby/E+/Getty Images, 47; Craig Lambert/iStock/Getty Images, 48; PaulWolf/iStock/Getty Images, 49; Fletcher Munsterman/Shutterstock, 50 (top); Cultura RF/Brett Phibbs/Connect Images/Getty Images, 50 (bottom); eco2drew/iStock/Getty Images, 51; Cyril di Bisceglie/Wikimedia Commons, 52; by wildestanimal/Moment/Getty Images, 53, 99; VWPics/Gerard Lacz/Blue Planet Archive, 54–55; Martin Ruegner/Stone/Getty Images, 55; Ahturner/Shutterstock, 56; Reinhard Mink/Moment/Getty Images, 57; Auscape/Universal Images Group/Getty Images, 58 (top), 72, 73, 119 (top), 186 (middle); Ken Griffiths/Shutterstock, 58 (bottom), 66, 81, 110, 112, 117, 118 (middle), 143, 175; Grant Mitchell Photos/Shutterstock, 59 (top); Kristian Bell/Shutterstock, 59 (middle); Wright Out There/Shutterstock, 59 (bottom); Images from BarbAnna/Moment/Getty Images, 60; James R.D. Scott/Moment/Getty Images, 61 (bottom), 98; Michele Jackson/iStock/Getty Images, 62; Kevin Wells/iStock/Getty Images, 63; DianaLynne/iStock/Getty Images, 64; Alexander Machulskiy/Shutterstock, 65; Ken Griffiths/iStock/Getty Images, 67, 69 (top), 69 (bottom), 76, 83, 88, 95, 106, 107, 113, 114 (top), 114 (bottom), 115, 119 (bottom); Windzepher/iStock/Getty Images, 68; media-ceh/Shutterstock, 70–71; Irina Babina/iStock/Getty Images, 74; vkp-australia/iStock/Getty Images, 75; Philip Thurston/E+/Getty Images, 77 (top); Byronsdad/E+/Getty Images, 77 (bottom); Marc Dozier/The Image Bank/Getty Images, 78; treetstreet/iStock/Getty Images, 79; Imogen Warren/iStock/Getty Images, 80, 145 (top); KarenHBlack/iStock/Getty Images, 84; Imogen Warren/Shutterstock, 85, 121, 178; Illia Khurtin/Shutterstock, 89; Uwe-Bergwitz/iStock/Getty Images, 90–91; PauloResende/iStock/Getty Images, 92; Frank Teigler/Premium Stock Photography GmbH/Alamy, 93; EAGiven/iStock/Getty Images, 96; SeanScottPhotography/Shutterstock, 97; Norbert Probst/imageBROKER/Getty Images, 100; Kryssia Campos/Moment/Getty Images, 101; reptiles4all/Shutterstock, 102–103, 105; aussiesnakes/iStock/Getty Images, 104; Steven Tessy/iStock/Getty Images, 108–109; Paul Biris/Moment/Getty Images, 109; Trevor Charles Graham/Shutterstock, 111; NickEvansKZN/Shutterstock, 116; Jason Edwards/The Image Bank/Getty Images, 118 (top); Eric Isselee/Shutterstock, 118 (bottom); Patrick Honan/iStock/Getty Images, 119 (middle); drferry/iStock/Getty Images, 122; Foxtrot Sierra/Shutterstock, 123 (top); asiafoto/iStock/Getty Images, 123 (bottom); Henry Cook/iStock/Getty Images, 124; nmulconray/Moment/Getty Images, 125; tracielouise/iStock/Getty Images, 126, 133; Ian Lumsden/500px/Getty Images, 127; kristianbell/RooM/Getty Images, 129; munro1/iStock/Getty Images, 130; Banu R/iStock/Getty Images, 131; Resolock/Shutterstock, 132 (top); photomaster/Shutterstock, 132 (bottom); photographereddie/iStock/Getty Images, 134; Klaus Hollitzer/iStock/Getty Images, 135; imageBROKER/Jurgen & Christine Sohns/Getty Images, 136; fluffandshutter/iStock/Getty Images, 137; Javier Fernández Sánchez/Moment/Getty Images, 138; Imagevixen/RooM/Getty Images, 141; Chasing Light - Photography by James Stone james-stone.com/Moment/Getty Images, 142 (top); tim phillips photos/Moment/Getty Images, 142 (bottom); Photography by Rob D/Shutterstock, 144 (top); Arun Sankaragal/Shutterstock, 144 (bottom left); kmn sandamali/Shutterstock, 144 (bottom right); Michal Pesata/Shutterstock, 145 (bottom); imageBROKER/Norbert Probst/Getty Images, 146; powerofforever/E+/Getty Images, 147; Katherine Obrien/iStock/Getty Images, 149; Kevin Boutwell/Moment/Getty Images, 150; SnBence/iStock/Getty Images, 151; Sahara Frost/Shutterstock, 152, 170 (bottom); Dirk van der Heide/Shutterstock, 153; Colin_Davis/iStock/Getty Images, 155; Philip Thurston/iStock/Getty Images, 156; michaelgeyer_photography/Shutterstock, 158; Mayumi.K.Photography/Shutterstock, 159; Howard Chen/iStock/Getty Images, 161, 166; Ken Kiefer 2/Connect Images/Getty Images, 162; Vladimir Mladenovic/E+/Getty Images, 164; Rixipix/iStock/Getty Images, 165; Lois_McCleary/iStock/Getty Images, 167; crisod/iStock/Getty Images, 168–169; Anna Azimi/Shutterstock, 170 (top); Hal Beral/Corbis/Getty Images, 170 (middle); Nigel Marsh/iStock/Getty Images, 171 (top); KarenHBlack/Shutterstock, 171 (middle); Velvetfish/iStock/Getty Images, 171 (bottom); DMVPhotography/iStock/Getty Images, 172; Daniel Mertes/Shutterstock, 172–173; MarieHolding/iStock/Getty Images, 174; chilterngreen.de/Shutterstock, 176; whitejellybeans/Shutterstock, 177 (top); Reinhard Dirscherl/ullstein bild/Getty Images, 177 (bottom); skydie/iStock/Getty Images, 179; Gilles MARTIN/Gamma-Rapho/Getty Images, 180; ViniSouza128/iStock/Getty Images, 181; Mark Newman/iStock/Getty Images, 182; electra/Shutterstock, 183 (top); Tatevosian Yana/Shutterstock, 183 (bottom); Louise Docker Sydney Australia/Moment/Getty Images, 184 (top); Robbie Goodall/Moment/Getty Images, 184 (bottom); ChameleonsEye/Shutterstock, 185; Robin Bush/Photodisc/Getty Images, 186 (top); Dorling Kindersley/Universal Images Group/Newscom, 186 (bottom); Brittany North/Shutterstock, 187 (top); yod 67/Shutterstock, 187 (middle); Pong Wira/Shutterstock, 187 (bottom)

ABDOBOOKS.COM

Published by Abdo Reference, a division of ABDO, PO Box 398166, Minneapolis, Minnesota 55439. Copyright © 2026 by Abdo Consulting Group, Inc. International copyrights reserved in all countries. No part of this book may be reproduced in any form without written permission from the publisher. Encyclopedias™ is a trademark and logo of Abdo Reference.

Printed in China
052025
092025

Editor: Jane Katirgis
Series Designer: Colleen McLaren

LIBRARY OF CONGRESS CONTROL NUMBER: 2024948998

PUBLISHER'S CATALOGING-IN-PUBLICATION DATA
Names: Gramson, Hannah, author.
Title: The Australian animal encyclopedia / by Hannah Gramson
Description: Minneapolis, Minnesota : Abdo Reference, 2026 | Series: Animal encyclopedias | Includes online resources and index.
Identifiers: ISBN 9781098296605 (lib. bdg.) | ISBN 9798384918035 (ebook)
Subjects: LCSH: Zoology--Australia--Juvenile literature. | Animals--Juvenile literature. | Animals--Behavior--Juvenile literature. | Animal habitats--Juvenile literature. | Reference materials--Juvenile literature. | Encyclopedias and dictionaries--Juvenile literature.
Classification: DDC 590.3--dc23